Outlines

MORRISSEY

Other works by Pat Reid
Bigmouth: Morrissey 1983-1993
(The Dunce Directive, 1993)
20th Century Icons: Rock and Pop
(Absolute Press, 2001)
20th Century Icons: Gay
(Absolute Press, 2001)

Outlines

MORRISSEY

PAT REID

Absolute Press

First published in 2004 by

Absolute Press
Scarborough House,
29 James Street West,
Bath, England BA1 2BT
Phone 01225 316013
Fax 01225 445836
E-mail outlines@absolutepress.co.uk
Web www.absolutepress.co.uk

Series editor Nick Drake

Printed by Legoprint, Italy

ISBN 1 899791 73 6

Contents

MORRISSEY TRIUMPHANTLY WIELDS HIS BOUQUET OF BARBS DURING THE EARLY
DAYS OF THE SMITHS' SUCCESS.

One

Whether you care or do not[1]

Morrissey is forever singing about himself, or different versions of himself, at any rate. 'The more you ignore me, the closer I get,' he trilled in 1993. As it happened, the more the public ignored him, the further away he got. Morrissey, he who once had given a good account of himself in commercial terms against '80s giants Michael Jackson, U2, Madonna and Bruce Springsteen, finally came unstuck in the '90s.[2] The Spice Girls walked all over him. It wasn't really the fault of his music, though. 'The More You Ignore Me' was typically enigmatic, although infuriatingly slight, as many of his singles would be throughout the '90s (In 2000 it was used, bizarrely, in a self-aggrandising TV show that Posh Spice made about herself, soundtracking a sequence where the skeletal Mrs Beckham walked around a supermarket to test whether the public would recognise her). Creatively, however, Morrissey was far from finished. Buried among the extra tracks on his CD singles, lost in the grooves of those unfancied albums, would be songs of real merit, lyrics that caressed and bit as much as his finest work with The Smiths. But Morrissey seemed to be making it as hard as possible for people to be into him.

I still love him, though. When I told people this in 1991, I was on the defensive even then. Because, despite the large and still predominantly youthful audience he commanded, Morrissey was seen even at that point as an artist becoming an anachronism, a man slipping into self-parody.[3] When I

---

1   From 'The More You Ignore Me, The Closer I Get'.
2   Morrissey's record sales were far lower, of course, but in the pages of the UK music press, he ruled.
3   Johnny Marr, guitarist with The Smiths, reportedly feared that the band were turning into a caricature, 'like The Beach Boys, in striped shirts'.

started writing the essay that was later published as *Bigmouth: Morrissey 1983-1993*, it rapidly became clear that I was penning an apologia. I remember attending a Smiths and Morrissey night in London around that time. I enjoyed dancing to such a wide range of songs by my favourite artist, but I had misgivings about my fellow revellers. You really got the impression that these kids didn't listen to any other sort of music, that they lived their lives through Morrissey – that he was all they had. Maybe this shouldn't be an issue. After all, no one spends time worrying whether fans of Coldplay or Britney Spears listen to a wide and healthy cross-section of music. But to a pop-culture obsessive, and to anyone who considers himself or herself a functioning member of society, this is a crucial question. The limitations of your language are the limitations of your life. The same goes for your musical vocabulary.

The other reason why critics worried about the musical diets of Morrissey fans was precisely because Morrissey did appear to be so important. He is, I think, the greatest lyricist in the English language since the Second World War. Clearly, the English-language lyric is a neglected art, if not a dying one. And yet Morrissey remains the best we've got. He's probably had a more profound effect on British minds than any novelist, poet, playwright or film-maker of his generation.[4] By this I mean Morrissey is a serious artist, worthy of the kind of critical scrutiny usually reserved for poets like Ted Hughes or Philip Larkin, novelists such as Martin Amis, playwrights like Noel Coward and Joe Orton, or actors like John Gielgud and Laurence Olivier.

Between 1983 and 1993, Morrissey was a gigantic figure in the British cultural landscape. In retrospect, this was largely due to the coverage of long-running music weekly the *NME*, which lauded him in the '80s and attacked him in the '90s.[5] The paper was even partly responsible for the break-up of The Smiths in 1987, with News Editor Danny Kelly constructing a story about the band's demise which actually prompted their final ruction. After the *NME* tagged Morrissey as a racist in 1992, he refused to speak to them.[6]

---

4   Indeed, could anybody even name a notable film-maker from Morrissey's generation?
5   The *New Musical Express*, which celebrated its 50th anniversary in 2002. Long-term rival *The Melody Maker* closed the year before, shortly after its 75th anniversary.

In the April 2001 issue of *Mojo*, Morrissey pondered his former press adulation: 'Once you start riding on that wave, and the British press at last lets you in and lets you ride, it's an incredible feeling. And it lasted for five years...' The implication was that Morrissey now stood alone, and would always do so. Such a reciprocal relationship with the media could never happen again.

In 2003, however, it does seem painfully clear that the *NME*'s role in British and world popular culture has diminished significantly. It looks like Morrissey has won that particular scrap, merely by ignoring the paper and letting time take its course. Music and the media have changed beyond all recognition in the intervening decade, but Morrissey remains the same. Curiously, now that there seems to be no short-term prospect of new recordings, his aura is burning brightly once again.[7] This is partly because no one has ever fully replaced him. Morrissey has plenty of failings as a writer, singer and performer but, like some Daley Thompson of pop, he scores the most points overall, he takes his place on the podium.[8] Frontmen who found fame in his wake, like Damon Albarn, Kurt Cobain, Liam Gallagher, Jarvis Cocker and Richard Ashcroft – some of whom have since become sacred cows – have nevertheless failed to equal Morrissey's body of work.[9] At the other end of the spectrum, the mega-successful Robbie Williams is perhaps the ultimate pop star, but he is not, nor will ever be, an artist; Morrissey is, and will be forever.

6   In the infamous 'This Alarming Man' piece. A decade later *NME* staffer Andrew Collins was still boasting – possibly ironically – of having 'outed Morrissey as a Nazi'. Moving to *Select* magazine, Collins' next notable achievement was the 'Who Do You Think You Are Kidding, Mr Cobain?' Britpop-themed issue, which employed precisely the same Union Jack imagery for which Morrissey had been pilloried.

7   At the time of writing, the Morrissey fan grapevine is feverish with anticipation of new material; certainly, Morrissey has written many new songs, and recorded at least some of them.

8   Thompson was a UK decathlete, and hero of the 1980 and 1984 Olympics.

9   Respectively: vocalist and lyricist with Blur; guitarist, vocalist and lyricist with Nirvana; vocalist with Oasis; vocalist and lyricist with Pulp; vocalist and lyricist with The Verve.

Stretch out and wait

This is a book about Morrissey, his life, his music and his sexuality. Especially, perhaps, his sexuality, because it's that force which seems to colour just about everything he does, much as Madonna's sexuality influences her every move (albeit in a rather more obvious and immeasurably tackier way). Of course, Morrissey would deny this. As Johnny Rogan reported, when a writer famously referred to the 'vexed question of Morrissey's sexuality', the singer retorted with outrage, 'But who does it vex? It doesn't vex me.'[10]

For the length of his career Morrissey has claimed to be celibate. There were a few fumbling pre-fame relationships, and there have been hints of sporadic encounters since, but he is no Rod Stewart.[11] Most onlookers assume that Morrissey is by inclination gay or bisexual. My feeling is that, like Kenneth Williams, Morrissey finds it incredibly difficult and traumatic to come to terms with his desires, and is unable to form lasting relationships.[12] Whether or not he is reconciled to this, I don't know, but as his lyrics are almost exclusively about pain, loss, regret and alienation, I suspect not.

To the world, it appears that Morrissey has had no long-term partners.[13] To quote one of the tracks from the 1986 Smiths album *The Queen Is Dead*, he has, it seems, 'never had no one ever'. Either that, or his partners are incredibly loyal and/or principled – qualities conspicuous by their absence in the music world, where everyone has a price and where the telling usually begins mere moments after the kissing stops.

10   Author of the major biography *Morrissey & Marr: The Severed Alliance*, as well as *The Smiths: The Visual Documentary* and *The Complete Guide To The Music Of The Smiths & Morrissey/Marr*.

11   Frontman of The Faces and '70s solo star, famed for his lothario image and numerous leggy blonde conquests.

12   Williams (1926-1988) was a British character actor, humorist and star of the *Carry On* films. Despite his friendship with the unashamedly homosexual playwright Joe Orton, Williams was tormented by guilt over his sexuality.

13   The enigmatic figure of Jake, the 'best friend on the payroll' from the *Your Arsenal/ Vauxhall And I* years is possibly the exception here.

Again, my feeling is that Morrissey lives a solitary existence. 'I'm writing this to say in a gentle way, thank you but no,' he sings in the exquisite 1988 B-side 'Will Never Marry. 'I will live my life as I will undoubtedly die... alone'. In the first flush of his early '90s fame with Suede, Brett Anderson put forward an appealing theory that this lyric had perhaps started life as a reply to a piece of fan mail. Well, I wonder.

At any rate, it is apparent that people who have sex with musicians are very often compelled to tell the world about it. Morrissey, therefore, must choose his partners with extreme caution, or be in possession of some supernatural means of silencing them. Either that, or he has no partners.

The books that have been written about Morrissey – by the likes of Mick Middles, Johnny Rogan and myself – tend to be quite revealing about their authors. Morrissey has a way of bringing out that fanzine editor's obsessional devotion which is traditionally the enemy of objectivity. But I think it is important to reveal a little about myself and my interest in Morrissey. I am a heterosexual male in my early thirties. Born at the end of 1968, I grew up in a village north of Liverpool, 40 miles away from Morrissey's Manchester. My politics are broadly left-wing and I am not homophobic. And yet, in spite of my heterosexuality, my passion for Morrissey has always had a near-sexual dimension. This is not so unusual for pop fans. I once saw a film-maker commenting on '60s footage he shot of a stage invasion during a Rolling Stones performance at the Albert Hall. 'When those boys got on the stage,' he said. 'You could see that they wanted to kiss Mick Jagger'. Liverpool singer and former Morrissey associate Pete Burns commented about the early '70s days of glam rock and David Bowie's incarnation as Ziggy Stardust, 'You used to hear dockers saying, "Yeah, I'd give Bowie one". It was liberating'. I was reminded of this in the mid '90s while discussing Morrissey with a fellow music journalist: 'Me and all my mates are straight,' he told me, 'but we all agreed, "Yeah, Morrissey? I'd sleep with him."' At the time, Morrissey was at the peak of his powers as a sexually magnetic performer, and this was not an uncommon reaction among his heterosexual male followers. In sexual terms, male pop stars tend to be ambivalent creatures, daubed in make-up, hip-thrusting in the spotlight. When I saw

US pop culture professor Greil Marcus give a talk on Elvis Presley in the early '90s he said, 'In the 1950s half of America thought Elvis was the archetypal sexual predator, a threat to their daughters' morals; the other half though he was a degenerate homosexual.' Mick Jagger caused similar confusion in the 1960s: to some he was a satanic satyromaniac; to others he was nothing but a flouncing cissy – either way, they were outraged. The writer who gets closest to capturing the boundary-blurring passion of the heterosexual male pop fan for certain iconic artists is the late Lester Bangs. Describing his experience at an early '70s Elvis Presley concert in Las Vegas with characteristic honesty, he recalled: 'He was the only male performer I've ever reacted to sexually'.[14]

There is an all-girl heavy metal band called Rockbitch, who incorporate a hardcore sex show into their live act. In keeping with their pagan/feminist manifesto, they claim that all music is pornographic, and that they are simply being more honest than, say, Britney Spears. Morrissey is a good deal more subtle than Rockbitch, but he does it too. This is, after all, the man who regularly won the 'Most Beautiful Buttocks' award in *Record Mirror*'s annual readers' poll.

Interestingly, gay culture has always been ambivalent towards Morrissey. In the '80s, some gay activists were angered by Morrissey appropriating gay icons for Smiths sleeves, while refusing to come out and stand alongside them in the struggle for equality.[15] In more recent years, Morrissey has become an anathema to the upwardly mobile gay culture depicted in the popular Channel 4 series *Queer As Folk*, which followed the hedonistic adventures of the denizens of Manchester's Canal Street. These days, it seems, Morrissey is only a gay icon to straight men.

Well, a certain type of straight man, at any rate. When Suede emerged as natural successors to The Smiths in the early '90s, frontman Brett Anderson made the oft-quoted announcement that he considered himself to be a 'bisexual man who has never had a homosexual experience', expressing

---

14   From the Bangs collection *Psychotic Reactions And Carburettor Dung*.
15   See Johnny Rogan, *Morrissey And Marr: The Severed Alliance*.

something which, although much-ridiculed, was in fact keenly felt by a sizeable proportion of his – and Morrissey's – audiences.[16]

There are other problems with arguing that an artist's sexuality is the one crucial influence on their work. Neil Tennant of the Pet Shop Boys, the synth duo whose success in the '80s paralleled Morrissey's, came out in the early '90s and feels that, while this revelation seems to have won the band an increased gay following, the associations aren't always appropriate: 'I don't think your sexuality necessarily determines what you do musically,' he argues. In any case, no matter how sophisticated one's 'gaydar', there is simply no accurate way of determining that a particular lyric or piece of music is the work of a gay man. Or, for that matter, a celibate man. The old cliché about music being a universal language happens to be true.

One gay writer who still rates Morrissey highly is the estimable Mark Simpson. The founder and spokesman of the 'Anti-gay' movement, Mark believes gay culture has degenerated into a meaningless conveyor belt of hedonism, empty consumerism, and shallow, disposable music. I encountered Mark in 1991 when I was editing the special Morrissey issue of a student publication named *Outlook*, and I commissioned him to write about his experiences as a young Smiths fan. He delivered a heartfelt piece describing his road to Damascus moment at an open-air benefit for the Greater London Council that The Smiths played in 1985. It was a hot, sunny day and the young male fans stripped to the waist to dance their adoration of the band. 'The scales fell from my eyes,' Mark recalled, 'and I fell in love with the boys for being in love with Morrissey'.

And perhaps that is where Morrissey's true power resides. Like all real pop stars, he has the ability to make you fall in love with him. Over the course of the next fifteen years, other bands and artists would attain and even exceed the demented levels of devotion that Morrissey enjoyed – if devotion is the

---

16   After two strong albums, Suede guitarist Bernard Butler left the band in 1994. Without their 'Johnny Marr' figure, Suede never quite regained their initial momentum or creative edge.

correct word. The Stone Roses, The Happy Mondays, Suede, Nirvana, Blur, Oasis, Pulp and The Verve have all been there, but never with anything close to the peculiar combination of intellectual, sexual and emotional intensity reserved for Morrissey. In the same way that he still holds the record for selling out the Hollywood Bowl in the quickest time, and for doing the biggest ever in-store signing at HMV Manchester, Morrissey has yet to be knocked off that particular top spot.[17]

Paint a vulgar picture[18]

So is Morrissey still relevant today? After all, so much has happened in music, and in the wider world, to squeeze him out of the picture, to make his glory days seem a distant memory. The answer, however, is, yes, he is still relevant, if only because the intelligent, incisive lyric is a dying art, and because in 2003 the popular music of the English-speaking world has entered a state of corporate conservatism and artistic redundancy from which it may never recover. We need artists like Morrissey. Indeed, in this age of mercilessly-marketed kiddiepop, brain-dead nu-metal and conspicuous consumption-obsessed hip-hop, we need any real artists at all. In 1983, when The Smiths emerged, British teenagers weaned on *Grease*, *Saturday Night Fever* and Blondie, and nurtured by Duran Duran, Spandau Ballet and ABC, when finding themselves ready for adult material, could instantly tap into an entire sprawling alternative culture that encompassed music, fashion, journalism and politics. Today, there is nothing of the sort. Young people aged from eight to 28 seem content to stick with Britney Spears, perhaps graduating to 'safe' alternative-type bands like Coldplay, Travis and Stereophonics. The UK music press, while still a breeding ground for writing talent, is a toothless beast compared to the vibrant hydra of the '80s and early '90s. The only jot of vitality is in the 'metal' genre covered by magazines like *Kerrang* (although this publication is now

---

17   Incredibly, even Take That, the most successful UK boyband of the '90s, with strong Manchester links, did not attract as many fans.

18   'Paint A Vulgar Picture' is one of the key tracks from *Strangeways Here We Come*.

distancing itself from the term 'metal') and *Metal Hammer*.[19] In this realm, artists as diverse as Marilyn Manson and The Offspring find an audience for their ideas as well as their music. These publications are obliged to cover an awful lot of music which is either lame or too extreme for mass consumption, but they at least understand that music fans are receptive to much more from their favourite bands than their latest CD and tour T-shirt. Neither Manson nor The Offspring are musical or lyrical innovators, but both put on a good show, sell lots of CDs, beat the music industry at its own game and encourage their fans to think. Until their demise in 2000, the Smashing Pumpkins were perhaps the ultimate band for the thinking rock fan. Emerging from Chicago in the early '90s as grunge blossomed forth from Seattle to the west, the Pumpkins, under the despotic leadership of Billy Corgan, pioneered a brand of what was almost intellectual or avant-garde heavy metal. They were a world-class band, their material success far outstripping that of The Smiths and Morrissey. At their height in 1995-96, they sold ten million copies of the hugely ambitious double CD *Melon Collie And The Infinite Sadness*. If the suicide of Kurt Cobain had not conferred iconhood upon Nirvana, the Pumpkins would certainly have eclipsed their Seattle rivals. What Corgan has in common with Manson and The Offspring's Dexter Holland is the fact that, in their contrasting ways, all three take their positions as role models very seriously. In interviews they are intelligent and articulate, continually pushing their fans in the direction of music, movies, books, art and issues that may fuel their imaginations.[20] They use websites for the same ends. This may just mean that fans get to hear about the showbiz Satanism of Anton LaVey from Manson, or have an opportunity to ponder the arcane philosophies that fascinate Corgan, or follow up on Holland's recommendation that The Damned are a pretty neat band, but at least it proves that there is life outside the juggernaut of consumer culture that pop music has become.

19   Reflecting the fact that the UK alternative music scene has effectively been colonised by US rock acts, *Kerrang* overtook the *NME* in 2002 to become the world's biggest-selling music weekly.

20   Indeed, all three promote the ground-breaking British music of the punk and post-punk eras far more than any British artists do.

I remember reading a *Smash Hits* interview with Echo And The Bunnymen singer Ian McCulloch in 1983, around the time that the band's *Porcupines* album was released. The interviewer visited the singer at his home in Liverpool and witnessed Mac's girlfriend Lorraine cleaning out the cage of the couple's pet hamster. The hamster was named Hieronymous, after McCulloch's favourite painter, the medieval visionary Hieronymous Bosch. Lorraine referred to him as 'Hiroshima'. At the time, *Smash Hits* was Britain's biggest-selling pop title, covering the 'new pop' of Duran Duran and Culture Club, and yet it was perfectly acceptable for it to give its readers a nudge, however indirectly, in the direction of an artist famed for his nightmarish depictions of hell.[21] Today, when the glossy emptiness of kiddie-pop (with a smattering of UK garage) rules cool Britannia via daytime Radio 1, virtually all music outlets on TV, most major internet music newsletters and the print media (Destiny's Child and Hear'say on the cover of the *NME*, the same paper championing Sugababes as a 'great new band'), such dissemination of ideas, except, ironically, in the aforementioned metal mags for so long associated with music's dumbest, most reactionary genre, is almost non-existent.[22]

In their 1977 classic of amphetamine-gibberish punk journalism *The Boy Looked At Johnny*, Julie Burchill and Tony Parsons stated with characteristic

---

21   Neither would the meaning of the word 'Hiroshima' have been thought beyond the knowledge of a *Smash Hits* reader in 1983. To be fair, the magazine today has a much younger readership, but an infantile obsession with sexiness and snoggability reigns, and the artists featured are uniformly moronic, although fully complicit in the merciless exploitation of their teenage and pre-teen fans. Again I state that in the early '80s, pop musicians in general had a lot more to say for themselves, while the average pop fan was a good deal less dumb.

22   Radio 1 was launched in 1967. The BBC's pop music station has survived a turbulent period in the '90s and has now reasserted its place in UK music culture, where its dominance reflects that of MTV in other territories. In 2000 an industry insider told me that Radio 1 was considered the only avenue for breaking a new band in the UK. (Destiny's Child are a US R&B trio, led by the fearsomely ambitious Beyonce Knowles and specialising in militantly vacuous hardbody pop in the urban music genre; Hear'say were the winners of the UK's televised *Popstars* contest. Less than a year after their two million-selling debut single, the group were already has-beens. Sugababes are a manufactured schoolgirl pop trio, whose name underlines their

inverted snobbery that, 'The Stranglers were the only punk band with degrees but they were as thick as shit.' In retrospect, of course, it's obvious that The Stranglers, masterful purveyors of three-minute classics of psychedelic misogyny, were not really punks and were certainly not 'thick', but it's a revealing statement. Because, in the late '70s and early '80s it was still expected – demanded even – that musicians should possess intelligence, however untutored; that they should have ideas, opinions, something to say. Former GLC leader Ken Livingstone, '80s hate figure to the right-wing tabloids and today the Mayor Of London, once said on the Terry Wogan show that most politicians were 'pretty average' in the brains department.[23] This certainly goes for most musicians too, but God bless them, back in those days they really tried. Paul Weller, frontman of The Jam and the Style Council, namechecked writers from Shelley to Colin MacInnes and spouted socialist ideals; Spandau Ballet dabbled with the avant-garde, while Dexy's Midnight Runners took out full page advertisements in the music press as a soapbox for frontman Kevin Rowland's demented belief in both himself and the emotional truth of his band's music.[24] Post-punkers and new popsters alike were drunk on ideas. Ex-Japan frontman David Sylvian appropriated the title of 'Forbidden Colours' from Yukio Mishima and took it into the charts, in collaboration with Japanese composer Ryuichi Sakamoto.[25] The major UK pop star of '80 to '82, Adam Ant sounded off about '60s pop art, fetishism, tribal cultures and eighteenth-century dandies, and acted in a revival of Joe

management's aim to make them a more street-credible version of the commercially-redundant Spice Girls.)

23   The Smiths were famously booked to perform as musical guests on Terry Wogan's TV chat show. This was scuppered when Morrissey changed his mind and simply disappeared.

24   Weller was photographed with Paul Foote's book *Red Shelley*, which argued the case for the Romantic poet as radical thinker. MacInnes was the author of *Absolute Beginners*.

25   Mishima was a homosexual Japanese writer and nationalist. After staging a failed coup in 1970, he committed ritual suicide. His life is the subject of Paul Schrader's 1985 film *Mishima*. The song featured on the soundtrack to *Merry Christmas Mr Lawrence*. The film, directed by Ngaisa Oshima and based on a novel by Laurens Van Der Post, starred Sakamoto alongside David Bowie.

Orton's *Entertaining Mr Sloane* at the Manchester Royal Exchange in 1983. That same year, U2 released their breakthrough album *War*, containing 'Sunday Bloody Sunday', a song so inflammatory, given the situation in Northern Ireland, that it had to be prefigured onstage with the disclaimer, 'This song is not a rebel song.'

Today, British art is an ugly joke, a money-making exercise for wannabe popstars like Tracey Emin and Damien Hirst.[26] Back then, art was everywhere; its fingers strayed into the unlikeliest of pies. Critically despised at the time, if a band like Duran Duran emerged today with their combination of pop art, sci-fi, great tunes (their stated punk-meets-disco musical manifesto) and even greater hair, they would be seen as dangerously subversive avant-garde intellectuals. Maybe they always were.[27]

And of course, the King of ideas was Morrissey, although he came to the fore just at the time when pretty much everyone else was reverting to the dumb hedonism that had characterised rock for much of the '70s. When Morrissey found himself finally commanding attention, after years of struggle and under-achievement in Manchester, he was unstoppable.[28] Everything he did or said was peppered with salient references, many of them uniquely Morrisseyesque in nature. Musically, he could point his fans towards glam, punk and the British girl singers of the '60s. He turned us on to classic British kitchen-sink dramas of the '60s – films like *Saturday Night And Sunday Morning* and *Billy Liar*, and the novels they were adapted from.[29] Bear in mind that this stuff was not trendy; were it not for the bard of Stretford it might well have been forgotten altogether. And then there were the record sleeves. Every Smiths

26   Damien Hirst directed the video for Blur's 'Country House' single in 1995, and later made the hideous 'Vindaloo' football record with Blur's bassist Alex James.

27   Duran keyboardist Nick Rhodes released a book of his blurry polaroids. Spandau Ballet's Gary Kemp, later to star alongside his brother Martin in *The Krays*, quickly pointed out its obvious debt to Hockney.

28   In retrospect, Morrissey's long, dark apprenticeship of the soul was not really all that long. He was famous at 24. Compare this to Jarvis Cocker's twelve-year slog with Pulp, or the decade that Joe Orton spent on the dole (including a six-month stint in prison) before tasting success.

single and album featured one of Morrissey's endless stock of personal icons –
from Jean Marais, star of Cocteau's surrealist classic *Orphee*, to *Breakfast At
Tiffany's* author Truman Capote, to the more mainstream, but still fascinating
likes of James Dean, not to mention a plethora of English eccentrics. His
lyrics, meanwhile, pilfered everything from Shelagh Delaney's *A Taste Of
Honey* to a Sid James quip from *Carry On Cleo*. Music journalist Mark Ellen
once said of *Smash Hits'* gimmick of printing the lyrics to current hit singles
that, 'If you'd just heard 'White Man In Hammersmith Palais' by The Clash,
then you'd want to know all the words.' Having deciphered Joe Strummer's
account of his experience at a reggae concert, the chances are you might also
check out some of the artists he referred to in the song. In the same way, if
you'd heard 'Suffer Little Children' by The Smiths, it might well lead you to
Beyond Belief, in which playwright Emlyn Williams retold the story of the
Moors Murderers in the Northern realist style of contemporaries such as Alan
Sillitoe and Keith Waterhouse.[30] In dozens of little ways, Morrissey was
engaging the minds of his listeners. He gave us more than any other lyricist.

School

The early Morrissey was, in his way, as dizzyingly absolute in his anti-
establishment stance as the Sex Pistols. Johnny Rotten and co. didn't know
much about anything, but theirs was the inspired dumbness of all great rock
'n' roll, the holy stupidity against which the adult world simply cannot defend
itself. Morrissey was, of course, a lot brighter than the Pistols; rather than
merely lashing out at society and himself, he selected his targets more
carefully. At times, his themes could seem quite perverse: why was he –
clearly an intelligent spokesman for youth – saying that school was bad and

29 The former starring Albert Finney, adapted from the 1958 novel by Alan Sillitoe;
    the latter starring Tom Courtenay, adapted from the novel by Keith Waterhouse.
30 *Beyond Belief* was first published in 1967 and subtitled *A Chronicle Of Murder And Its
    Detection*. To the Morrissey fan, phrases from the lyrics to 'Suffer Little Children' are
    to be found embedded within the text. Also, Myra Hindley's sister and brother-in-law
    are frequently referred to as 'the Smiths'.

that he didn't want a job? Possibly, these were just such thrillingly naughty things to say that he couldn't help himself. But then, Morrissey's highly uncommon personality – and associated personality problems – ensured that he was virtually unemployable anyway, in spite of his formidable yet ill-disciplined intelligence. Famously, Morrissey did not prosper at school, where his mental resourcefulness was allowed to wither on the vine. If it still existed today, St Mary's in Stretford would be described as 'failing'; it would be publicly named and shamed by the Blairite politburo. If by some miracle it managed to be spared closure, its decrepit complement of teachers would be replaced by bright young things in a hurry to get results. This was not how it was in the '70s. As described to Johnny Rogan by contemporaries of Morrissey, the school was inexorably bleeding to death in the glam rock decade. While Led Zeppelin reigned like golden gods at the Continental Hyatt House and Bowie acted out starchild superman fantasies, Steven Morrissey was being 'emotionally sodomised' at St Mary's. Consequently, themes of Morrissey's troubled schooldays loom large on the first two Smiths albums, most notably on 'The Headmaster Ritual' and 'Barbarism Begins At Home' on *Meat Is Murder* (1985). Oddly, though, while the listener is never left in any doubt that the deeds described in the songs are bad things, the actual abuse detailed seems pretty mild. The marauding headmaster ('He does the military two-step down the nape of my neck') is creepy, but hardly demonic, while the punishment doled out in 'Barbarism' – 'a crack on the head is what you get for asking' – would hardly strike fear into the street children of Sao Paulo, cowering from death squads. Abuse, like poverty, is relative.

EVERY INCH THE '80s POP IDOL, WITH GUEST APPEARANCE BY PAUL WELLER.
MORRISSEY LATER RECORDED A PLAINTIVE VERSION OF WELLER'S
'THAT'S ENTERTAINMENT'.

Two

God, How Sex Implores You[31]

Right from the very first interview, Morrissey's sexuality was pinned and mounted like a butterfly.[32] It hasn't budged very far since. That first gushing Dave McCullough interview appeared in *Sounds* on 4 June 1983. Disturbingly, McCullough comments, 'The subject of child molesting crops up more than a few times in Smiths songs. They are hilarious lyrics.' This airily introduced a topic that no journalist would treat so lightly now. Presumably in the early '80s child abuse was one of those subjects, like rape in the '60s, that still provoked a largely sniggering response from an ignorant male population. At any rate, McCullough, a fervent early admirer of The Smiths, unwittingly sowed the seeds for a tabloid witch-hunt, which could have severely damaged or even destroyed the band in its first year.[33] For the record, the band's response is an unattributed quote from either Morrissey or Marr (probably the former): 'We do not condone child molesting. We have never molested a child.'[34]

Commenting on what he perceives as the band's 'aggressively sexual stance', McCullough provokes a contradictory response from Morrissey:

31   From 'Stretch Out And Wait'.
32   The line from 'Reel Around The Fountain' recalls the central character of John Fowles' *The Collector*, played by Terrence Stamp in the film adaptation.
33   A swift and decisive damage limitation action by Morrissey saved the band.
34   In recent years, glam rock king Gary Glitter has served a prison sentence for possessing child pornography, and pop impresario Jonathan King has been jailed for committing sexual offences against underage boys, both cases providing frightening glimpses into the dark underbelly of the music business.

'I'm in fact very anti-aggression. Obviously I'm interested in sex and every song is about sex. I'm very interested in gender. I feel I'm a kind of prophet for the fourth sex. The third sex, even that has been done and it's failed. All that Marc Almond bit is pathetic. It sounds trite in print but it's something close to "men's liberation" that I desire'.[35]

Heady stuff, but a manifesto that Morrissey was soon to ditch. Even in the phenomenally pretentious milieu of the early '80s music press, this was a bridge too far. What he was saying loud and clear, however, was 'We are here and it is now', spelling out the fact that The Smiths were different.[36] In the same interview, Morrissey name-checks feminist authors, describes feminism as 'an ideal state', applauds the gallows humour of Stevie Smith and Sylvia Plath, and celebrates unemployment (then a subject of grave national concern) with the words,

'Jobs reduce people to absolute stupidity, they forget to think about themselves. There's something so positive about unemployment. You won't get trapped into materialism, you won't buy things you don't really want.'[37]

Of course, another deep thinker, George Michael of Wham!, had said pretty much the same thing more than six months earlier in the seminally subversive

35   Could McCulloch's description of The Smiths have been more inaccurate? Even then, onlookers felt that McCulloch was projecting his own notions of what The Smiths should be on to the band. Marc Almond was born in the north-west seaside town of Southport (alluded to in Morrissey's *Southpaw Grammar* album title). He fronted the arty synth duo Soft Cell, whose reworking of 'Tainted Love' was the biggest hit single of 1981. By 1983, he was viewed as an effete teenybopper joke by many serious critics, and yet his ongoing personal and musical explorations of the dark side would provide much fine work. *Men's Liberation* was the title of a book by Jack Nichols, which was influential in shaping Morrissey's views on identity and gender politics.

36   A quote from *Men's Liberation* that Morrissey appropriated in the early '80s.

37   Smith was an English poet, best known for 'Not Waving, But Drowning', recalled in Morrissey's 'Lifeguard Sleeping, Girl Drowning' from *Vauxhall And I*. Plath was an American poet and the wife of poet laureate Ted Hughes. She committed suicide in 1963. Her posthumous volume *Ariel* remains required reading for depressed students everywhere. Her gravestone in Hebden Bridge, Yorkshire, was regularly vandalised by feminists seeking to reclaim her memory from Hughes.

'Wham! Rap': 'I may not have a job / But I have a good time / With the boys that I meet / Down on the line.'[38] Morrissey ended his first real taste of media on a typically foppish note: 'We genuinely want a handsome audience above everything else.'

The Sun Shines Out Of Our Behinds[39]

Sex, then, was very much on the agenda for Morrissey and The Smiths, which may seem less than sensational now, but was rather more controversial in the early '80s. After the liberation of the '60s and the outright decadence of the '70s, rather more puritanical winds were blowing through the United Kingdom. With economic recession, mass unemployment and a music scene largely dominated by men posing as robots, sex was by no means as prevalent as it was today.[40] There were no 'lad mags', people were less tolerant of pornography, and were generally much less body conscious. Lap dancing clubs would not arrive for another decade or so and there were no lesbian kisses on soap operas. Indeed, there were no lesbians anywhere, or so it seemed. It was a well-known fact that the pop business was rife with homosexuality, but homosexuality itself was a dark continent to most people.[41] Indeed, homosexual acts between consenting adults had been legal in Britain for a mere 15 years. Chillingly, the first cases of AIDS were beginning to be

38   The subject of an embarrassed, although illuminating, biography by Johnny Rogan, Wham! were the UK's biggest pop duo of the '80s. They scored their first faux-rebellious pop-rap hits in 1982, enjoyed four of the biggest hit singles of 1984, and disbanded in 1986 with a concert at Wembley Stadium. George Michael went on to enjoy solo stardom, was the subject of a slavish official biography by Tony Parsons, and finally admitted to being gay after being arrested for indecent behaviour in a public lavatory in LA in 1998, an incident which he survived on a wave of public warmth.

39   From 'Hand In Glove'.

40   These robots were German electronic music pioneers Kraftwerk, who belatedly scored a UK number one hit with 'The Model' in 1982. By this time their sounds and concepts had become surprisingly commercial.

41   Boy George charmingly deflected questions about his sex life by claiming that he'd 'rather have a cup of tea'. His friend, and fellow 'gender-bender' Marilyn claimed, 'I've only slept with about ten people in my life. I don't consider that particularly promiscuous.'

reported, an event that would have a profound effect on the sexual life of anyone, straight or gay, who came of age in the mid-to-late '80s.[42]

How strange, then, that the man who claimed to never have sex was also the man who did more than any other to open up discussion and awareness of sex in the '80s via the medium of music.

Sex was evident right from the very first sleeve that Morrissey conceived and approved for The Smiths' debut single, 'Hand In Glove', in May 1983. As Jo Slee recalled, the image of undulating male buttocks culled from an unknown source sent a 'frisson of semi-homophobic delight through even the most earnest denizens of the Rough Trade offices'.[43] In case it needs pointing out, Rough Trade itself is gay slang for a tough, lower-class pick-up. As Rogan notes of 'Hand In Glove', 'The words proved equally appealing to star-crossed lovers, budding adolescent romantics and yet to be declared homosexuals'. Certainly, Morrissey's lyrical and vocal desperation are redolent of the love that dare not speak its name (and remember, this was still quite a big deal in 1983): 'We may be hidden by rags / But we've something they'll never have.' Of the famous sleeve, Morrissey quipped, 'Men need a better sense of their own bodies. Naked men should be splashed around the Co-op.'[44]

There's More To Life Than Books, Boy[45]

There were a number of articulate rock spokesmen at large in the early '80s; Elvis Costello, Julian Cope, Nick Cave and Joe Strummer among them. Morrissey, though, entered the fray at the age of 24 as a fully-formed human

---

42   The music press announced the AIDS-related deaths of avant-garde musician
      Klaus Nomi and disco producer Patrick Cowley in 1983.
43   In 2001, Rough Trade's fortunes were finally revived by New York band The
      Strokes. The cover of their debut album, *Is This It*, underlines their manly credentials
      by depicting a female backside stroked by a PVC glove.
44   Perhaps unconsciously, Morrissey is here echoing and subverting a line from 'A Town
      Called Malice' by The Jam, a much-loved number one in 1982.
45   From 'Handsome Devil'.

quote machine of the highest order. Unlike Ian McCulloch – nicknamed 'Mac the mouth' – of Echo and the Bunnymen, who merely said outrageous things in order to get a reaction and generally came off looking nasty and somewhat reactionary, Morrissey had his onstage and offstage persona worked out to a tee. In print he professed his admiration for Howard Devoto, a fellow Mancunian and leader of first The Buzzcocks and later Magazine, for having 'sat down and worked out what he was going to do beforehand'.[46] Like Morrissey, Devoto was an outsider, a dry, awkward man of indeterminate sexuality, possessed of a brittle sense of humour. 'I know he formed a group in order to make friends.' explained Morrissey. 'He'd never had any. I can only say I'm the same.' Morrissey was also friendly with Buzzcocks manager Richard Boon, a key figure on the late '70s Manchester punk scene. Boon had ties with Ludus, the band fronted by the formidable Linder. She and Morrissey would share an interest in feminist authors, a flat in Manchester's Whalley Range district, and a friendship, which, seemingly unique among Morrissey's relationships, has endured for more than 20 years. Linder took the venerational, homoerotic photographs of the 1991 tour that were published as *Morrissey Shot*. Her partner, the urbane novelist Michael Bracewell, supplied the introduction. In November 1999, Bracewell wrote a perceptive piece about Morrissey for *The Sunday Times* (with photographs by Linder), in which the singer welcomed him into his Hollywood home. Michael Bracewell is probably one of very few people with a good idea of what really makes Morrissey tick, as well as the equipment necessary to articulate it. Sadly, like everyone close to Morrissey, he gives very little away. 'There's really nothing there.' he told Dave Simpson of *Uncut* in 1998. 'I think the closest comparison is with Warhol. His power stems from a concentrated emptiness.'[47] Plausible, perhaps; tantalising, certainly. But very obviously not true.

46   In 2002 Devoto made a cameo appearance as a toilet cleaner in the film
      24 Hour Party People, which documents the Manchester music scene from 1976–92.
47   Despite taking its title from 'Still Ill' by The Smiths, Bracewell's 1997 book *England Is
      Mine: Pop Life In Albion From Wilde To Goldie*, is almost pathological in its avoidance of
      Morrissey, whose work is sprinted through in a few pages towards the end. Drum 'n'
      bass originator Goldie, whose image adorns the book's cover alongside Oscar Wilde,
      barely features at all.

The Human Ashtray

The post-punk dawn which greeted Morrissey in late '70s Manchester was alive with possibilities. While attempting to find a niche as a singer, the young 'Steve' Morrissey found himself writing for punk fanzines and then supplying a few short pieces to *Record Mirror* under the pseudonym Sheridan Whitehead. He had always written, of course: reputedly, he penned prospective scripts for *Coronation Street* as a youngster; in his teens he bombarded the music press with letters, a number of which were published; he also had numerous penfriends with whom he kept up a burgeoning correspondence.[48] By 1981, Morrissey was up to the task of authoring a slim volume on the New York Dolls, published by the tiny Babylon Books imprint. Two years later, Babylon released his second opus, *James Dean Is Not Dead*. Morrissey the author was actually pretty good. Wildly undisciplined, yet brimming with fanzine kid passion and excitement, he was probably influenced by such famed *NME* scribes as Charles Shaar Murray, Nick Kent, Tony Parsons and Julie Burchill, along with a smattering of stateside luminaries such as the substance dustbin music freak Lester Bangs, gonzo god Hunter S. Thompson, and New Journalism heavyweight Tom Wolfe. Had The Smiths never happened, Morrissey would probably have evolved further as a writer and pop culture historian. Another Mick Middles, or maybe a Paul Morley.[49]

Reading his two books now, the style may be awkward and dated, but they contain plenty of good stuff. Morrissey chose two icons that had helped shape his worldview. Dean was the 'tough kid who sometimes sleeps on nails', to use the phrase that Morrissey borrowed from director Howard Sachler's description of Dean for 'I Want The One I Can't Have'. Dean was also a timeless outsider whose car-smash death at 24 turned him into what Morrissey

48   *Coronation Street* is a long-running soap opera set in a working class community in Manchester.
49   Mick Middles published the first book on The Smiths in 1985. He was dismissed by Morrissey as 'Mick Muddled'.

described as 'the symbolic figure of the '50s'. If you believe *Hollywood Babylon II*, Dean was also a masochistic bisexual, constantly afflicted with the itch of crabs. Morrissey did not shy away from such allegations: 'It was rumoured far too frequently that he worked his way up trousers down. Had Warners, on signing Dean, bought and destroyed the porn movies which showed their precious protégé stripped for action?' *Hollywood Babylon II* asserts that Dean's party piece was approaching men at Hollywood gay bars and asking them to stub out their cigarettes on his chest, thereby earning himself the nickname 'The Human Ashtray'. Compiled by underground filmmaker, occultist and sexual adventurer Kenneth Anger, the *Hollywood Babylon* books were a compendium of the dark mythologies that festered in the belly of the Hollywood dream machine. Morrissey was almost certainly aware of them, as his writing, especially in his notes for *Exit Smiling*, an unfinished work on the morbid subject of Hollywood deaths, shows signs of having been influenced by Anger.

Morrissey's fixation with Dean was as complex as Dean himself. As fascinated with the lurid sexual details of Dean's life as so many are with the mysteries that lurk within the world of Morrissey, he noted the 'homosexual overtones' of the bedroom scene between Dean and Richard Davalos in *East of Eden*, and quoted Julie Harris' recollection of Dean reciting, 'The Lord is my Shepherd, I shall not suck cock', in a successful attempt to outrage Raymond Massey, the bible-loving actor playing his father.[50]

Revealingly, Morrissey described Dean as 'strong enough to be gentle', a line which he later adapted for one of his greatest songs, 'I Know It's Over' from *The Queen Is Dead*: 'It's so easy to laugh/ It's so easy to hate/ It takes guts to be gentle and kind.'

But perhaps most telling is Morrissey's account of the incredible levels of fan worship which Dean inspired after his premature death: 'Fan mail addressed to the corpse outnumbered that of any living Hollywood star', he claims. The mania Dean inspired posthumously is not so distant from that which Morrissey

---

50   Davalos later became cover star of the final Smiths studio album *Strangeways Here We Come*.

has himself generated during his own lifetime. Fans were alleged to have killed themselves after Dean's demise, just as they are alleged to have done after The Smiths split up (more recently, there were similar suicides following the self-inflicted death of Kurt Cobain); fans proclaimed themselves to be in touch with Dean in the hereafter; others besieged his family home in Fairmount, Indiana.[51] Morrissey goes on to paint a vulgar picture of the tacky exploitation that followed when the world found a dead star on its hands:

> '*Dean's wrecked Porsche was put on public display, and fans were invited, for a fee, to sit in the seat where he had died. For a little extra they were allowed to touch the dried blood on the steering wheel.*'[52] *Screw magazine, in a fitting gesture, proudly published pictures of the dead star naked.*'[53]

On a smaller scale, it's precisely this dangerously potent mixture of veneration and desecration that Morrissey has received – and even courted – throughout his career as a pop star.

Personality Crisis, Got It While It Was Hot[54]

If James Dean taught Morrissey what it is to be unconditionally loved, the New York Dolls showed him the value of outrage. As Lenny Kaye of the Patti Smith Group once said, 'Maybe we were the last of the '60s groups... and the Dolls were the first of the '70s groups.'[55] It's an accurate observation:

---

51   Morrissey himself visited Fairmount in 1988 to film the exquisitely moving Dean-homage video for 'Suedehead'.

52   In another macabre twist, British actor Alec Guinness was said to have had a premonition that Dean would die at the wheel of his car.

53   In 2002, within hours of her death in a car crash, a mortuary photograph of the child-like rapper Lisa 'Left Eye' Lopes was being circulated on the internet. Like James Dean, the early rocker Eddie Cochran – hugely influential in Britain – also died in a car crash, as did Morrissey's teenage idol Marc Bolan. The poignant 'Paint A Vulgar Picture', from *Strangeways Here We Come*, deals with the way in which the music industry exploits the deaths of its artists.

54   From 'Personality Crisis' by the New York Dolls.

55   Kaye was a guitarist, producer and rock anthologist.

Patti Smith, another of Morrissey's great icons, was a true artist; a poet with an unfailing belief in the power of rock 'n' roll to elicit social change, her alliances with the playwright/actor Sam Shepard and the subversively homosexual photographer Robert Mappelthorpe were testimony to the richness of her creative reserves. The Dolls, on the other hand, were pure whores. Festooned in the tackiest glam drag ever seen, they were a crew of New York reprobates who cared only for making a hideous noise, taking as many drugs as possible, and having sex with the kind of hotpant-clad jailbait that thronged around them at glam dives such as Rodney Bingenheimer's English Disco on LA's Sunset Strip.[56] In short, the Dolls were one of the most exciting happenings in the history of rock music. Like many British music fans, Morrissey, then 13, saw the Dolls on the BBC rock programme *The Old Grey Whistle Test*. He was instantly enamoured, and convinced he had witnessed an epochal event. Echoing Lenny Kaye, he proclaimed the Dolls 'the official end of the '60s'. *Whistle Test* covered a wide range of music, yet it is most remembered for presenter Bob Harris's preference for ponderous progressive rock. As the Dolls teetered off, Harris famously quipped 'Mock rock', thereby outraging such instant Dolls converts as Adam Ant, Mark E. Smith and the future members of the Sex Pistols. The Dolls were immensely influential in the UK. Before finding fame with The Clash, Mick Jones was, like the young Steven Morrissey, a huge fan of Mott The Hoople.[57] He subsequently came under the influence of the Dolls, who became the most significant ingredient in his seminal pre-punk band London SS. Adam Ant too recalled witnessing The Dolls at Wembley, where they supported the more conventional – and more successful – flash yobs Rod Stewart and the Faces. 'They just emptied the place,' Ant said years later, 'and I stood there watching them'. Another Dolls devotee was Nick Kent, the impossibly glamorous *NME* writer who briefly played guitar in an early line-up of the Sex Pistols. A few years later, punk, possibly the most significant cultural event of the '70s,

56   For an exploration of the LA glam scene see Barney Hoskyns, *Waiting For The Sun*.
57   Led by the Dylan-influenced Ian Hunter (author of *Diary Of A Rock 'n' roll Star*), Mott had actually split up when David Bowie rallied to their cause and bequeathed them an archetypal glam anthem with his song 'All The Young Dudes' in 1972. The young Steven Morrissey was a member of their fan club.

would owe a massive debt to the band that Morrissey later described, with a Kent-esque flourish, as 'high school toughs posing as bisexual psychopaths'.

Looking For A Kiss[58]

Fronted by rentaquote Mick Jagger doppelganger David Johansen ('Middle-class Catholic. Previous groups: Fast Eddie & The Electric Japs[59]'), and guitarist Johnny Thunders ('Real name: John Gonzales. Unabashed Italian with the largest supply of hair in rock history. Natural flair for perpetual collapsibility'), the Dolls made two albums, which didn't sell well enough to keep the band on the Phonogram label, and yet electrified thousands of freaks on both sides of the Atlantic.

Morrissey was absolute in his devotion to the band and their music. 'Their songs were much closer to home than most of the period,' he wrote in *New York Dolls*. 'They were bitter ('Vietnamese Baby'), urban ('Subway Train'), self-applauding and a little polluted. They sang about what they knew best – the bleak realities of ordinariness'. This last part, it must be said, sounds nothing like the Dolls, who possessed a remarkable talent for transforming any two chords into a veritable Mardi Gras. It does, however, closely resemble what Morrissey attempted to do just months later with The Smiths.

They might not have been on first-name terms with reality, but the Dolls were a miniature socio-sexual revolution in themselves. 'We want to form our own society,' Johansen declared, 'a society where everyone is on common ground. Everyone is alright with us'. Again, this was echoed and later surpassed in the 'Smiths nation' that rapidly coalesced around Morrissey in the mid-'80s. Morrissey noted, 'And, as always, the Dolls' sexuality needed clarification.' It was, of course, widely assumed that the Dolls were rampant homosexuals, due to their excessive trashiness. And yet, as Morrissey sniffily pointed out, 'That the Dolls were excessive womanisers was universal knowledge.' Morrissey goes on to quote extensively from the sexual philosophy of the ever-effusive

58   Another Dolls song title.
59   From a Dolls press release reproduced in Morrissey's book.

Johansen: 'Kids are finding out that there isn't much difference between them sexually. They're finding out that the sexual terms, homosexual, heterosexual, bisexual, all those are just words in front of "sexual". They accuse me of transsexuality because I kissed Jerry (Dolls drummer Jerry Nolan), but I love Jerry. I kiss him all the time. I think boys should kiss boys, don't you?'[60]

By the time the Dolls blasted into his universe, Morrissey had already nursed an infatuation with Marc Bolan, the elfin Earl of UK glam, had seen both Bolan and Bowie in concert, and would certainly have been aware of the sensational 'coming out' interview that Bowie gave to the *Melody Maker* in January 1972.[61] And yet, the Dolls were perhaps his greatest musical epiphany. 'Their influence upon what would happen in 1976 with the Sex Pistols cannot be emphasised enough.' he wrote. 'They dressed ambisexually not as a political statement but simply to show that they at least had the ability to laugh at themselves. The Dolls were never serious.'

Like so many wannabe rock stars of the mid-'70s, Morrissey started out by attempting to imitate the Dolls. It's to his credit that not a single note of the music he subsequently made, nor any syllable of his lyrical content, could lead even the most perceptive pop historian to suspect that this was the work of the most devoted fan the New York Dolls ever had. Musically, the chief legacy of the Dolls was not punk but the ghastly 'hair metal' that dominated US rock in the '80s. And yet Morrissey pays them tribute in the *Live In Dallas* video, filmed at his concert there in 1991. Flinging himself down on one knee like an imploring courtier, he leads his band through a version of the Dolls' 'Trash' that is pure Americana, evoking a lost world of gang rumbles, street corner doo-wop, unrequited love. Such things as stars are made of.

60   Both Johansen and his critics betray a fundamental misunderstanding of the term 'transsexual' here.
61   The astonishing David Bowie is certainly the greatest star – and most complete artist – that British pop music has ever produced. By 1972, still aged only 24, he was already a show business veteran, having adopted and discarded numerous identities in his quest for success. If Morrissey first heard the gay slang he quoted in 'Piccadilly Palare' in '60s wireless programmes like *Beyond Our Ken* and *Round The Horne* (Bona Drag being the name of a clothes shop opened by Julian and Sandy), then Bowie was certainly the first – and only – pop star to use terms like 'bona' (meaning 'good' or 'nice') in interviews.

MORRISSEY AND MARR: THE BEST SONGWRITING PARTNERSHIP OF THE '80S?
WE THINK SO.

Three

Oye! Esteban![62]

(E-mail from Simon Braund, West Coast Editor, *Empire* magazine, 5 May 2001)

Pat,

Let's be perfectly clear on this – you met and spoke to James Ellroy. You fucking tosser. The closest I've come is a signed copy of My Dark Places, *probably one of about 50,000 into which he idly scribbled his signature while watching Jerry Springer.*

You do realize, Morrissey's fan base being what it is these days, that if you do a reading in LA it's going to be in Compton or Watts?[63] I don't think they have too many branches of Barnes & Noble down there. Although I have to be honest and admit I've not been to check recently. Going to the beach now.

Best, Simon

James Ellroy has been my favourite author since I picked up a battered copy of *The Black Dahlia* which I found on the floor of the *Select* office in the summer of 1996. After the muscular noir of his *LA Quartet*[64], Ellroy has

---

62   Literally, 'Hey! Steven!', this has become quite a catchphrase among US Morrissey fans. Giving its name to a tour, a DVD and a popular Morrissey website, it underlines Morrissey's huge popularity in the Mexican–American community.

63   Compton, the predominantly-black area of Los Angeles, was immortalised by rap group Niggers With Attitude in the title of their 1990 album *Straight Out Of Compton*. Watts was a hotbed of Black Panther activism in the '60s and was a flashpoint for severe rioting in 1965, and again after the assassination of Martin Luther King in 1968.

abandoned the crime genre in favour of a style which allows him to construct an alternative history of the USA.

> *'If I were to write a contemporary LA crime novel,' he says, 'I wouldn't know how. I don't know LA any more – it's mainly non-Caucasian now, and I live with my wife in the white trash enclave of Kansas City.'*

When Ellroy comes to Bath on his UK tour in May 2001, promoting his new novel *The Cold Six Thousand* with a reading in Waterstones, I'm there. As he puts on his usual show ('Welcome, punks, prowlers, pederasts, panty-sniffers and pimps. You are going to be reamed, steamed and dry-cleaned.'), I find myself wondering if he has ever come across Morrissey. Born in LA in 1948, Ellroy would have been a perfect baby-boomer were it not for his profound dislike of the popular music of the '60s. However, despite his preference for what he terms 'bombastic German Romantic composers', Ellroy has at least some awareness of artists like Nick Cave and Tom Waits. Paul Morley once asked, 'Does Michael Jackson dream of the Cocteau Twins?'.[65] I find myself asking, does James Ellroy jive to 'You're The One For Me, Fatty' in Kansas City? I think not.

Certainly, it's interesting that while Ellroy has abandoned LA, a city which now bears little resemblance to the one that so fired his youthful mind and later inspired his best work, Morrissey has embraced it. Or rather LA has embraced Morrissey. Because this has been the single most significant occurrence of Morrissey's post-Smiths career – the manner in which his US fan base has been utterly transformed. And strangely, this appears to have happened largely along racial lines.

In 1999 *NME* Editor Steve Sutherland travelled to the Coachela Festival in Southern California, where Morrissey was appearing on a bill that included Beck and the Chemical Brothers. As Morrissey has refused to speak to the *NME* for many years, Sutherland, one presumes, was there to either do the

64   Sequentially, *The Black Dahlia*, *The Big Nowhere*, *White Jazz* and *L.A. Confidential*
65   In an essay in *Blitz* magazine in 1988.

usual hatchet job or to attempt to broker some form of rapprochement. No Morrissey interview ever came of it, but Sutherland was clearly impressed by what he saw. The 30,000 strong crowd that greeted Morrissey's performance were largely Hispanic in origin. The preponderance of Morrissey T-shirts confirmed that they weren't there for the Chemical Brothers. Morrissey had found a new audience. Interestingly, a couple of years earlier, the British band Gene, often dismissed as Smiths copyists, had told me that their best gigs had been in California, 'playing to thousands of Mexican kids in Gene T-shirts'. For some reason, it seems that sensitive intellectual English rock has found a new home.[66]

We Look To Los Angeles For The Language We Use[67]

While they tended to inspire complete contempt in your average Bon Jovi fan, to a certain kind of stateside hipster, The Smiths were always very trendy. You'd see references to them in Brat Pack novels by Brett Easton Ellis and Jay McInerney.[68] Lorna Luft, Judy Garland's other daughter, mentioned 'Girlfriend In A Coma' on a chat show. Microserfs author Douglas Coupland later co-opted it as the title of one of his none-more-*Generation X* books.[69] Multiple Oscar-winning actor Tom Hanks is supposedly a huge Morrissey fan.[70] Arch-rivals The Cure were, of course, also a massive cult in the states, while Depeche Mode, dismissed as lightweight synth-popsters in the UK, actually achieved a kind of gothic-electronic superstardom in America.[71] Not

---

66   In 2002 the Channel 4 youth programme *Passengers* devoted a small sequence to investigating Morrissey's popularity among Mexican-Americans in Los Angeles.

67   From 'Glamorous Glue'.

68   Respectively: author of *Less Than Zero* and *American Psycho* and author of *Bright Lights, Big City* and *Brightness Falls*.

69   Luft's half-sister is Liza Minnelli. *Girlfriend In A Coma* by Douglas Coupland was published in 1998.

70   Hanks is said to have requested to meet Morrissey after a concert, causing great embarrassment for the singer, who was not an admirer of the actor's work.

71   And in so doing they paved the way for the techno-industrial sound of Nine Inch Nails et al.

forgetting Morrissey's former bandmate Billy Duffy who, with The Cult, slugged it out in the heavy metal guitar hero premier league.[72] The Smiths, however, were always seen as the number one alternative band. Rough Trade boss Geoff Travis recalls that they were 'neck and neck with REM for years'. It wasn't until long after The Smiths had split that their counterparts from Athens, Georgia finally shifted up a gear and became one of the world's biggest bands. The Smiths were amazingly prolific in their short existence, but REM had the staying power. They acted more like a true democracy, they split songwriting credits four ways, and in Jefferson Holt, they had that holy grail of managers – the 'fifth member' who lives and breathes his band, and is totally at one with his charges. The Smiths sacked one manager after another, a pattern which has continued with Morrissey's solo career.

In Michael Stipe, of course, REM had a frontman possessed of an enigmatic charisma to rival Morrissey's. Unlike his Mancunian rival, however, Stipe seemed unconcerned with eclipsing his bandmates, and the REM unit seemed to be strengthened rather than weakened by the massive success they encountered in the '90s.[73] During this time, there were rumours of a fleeting emotional liaison between Stipe and Morrissey, the latter still speaking fondly of Stipe a decade later, and seemingly deeply grateful for the REM man's sole voice of support during his humiliating court case against Mike Joyce.[74] On the back of a strong comeback album, *Reveal*, in May 2001, Stipe finally declared that he was gay, the news creating rather less of a splash than REM guitarist Peter Buck's earlier arrest at Heathrow airport for alleged 'air rage' offences.

---

72   Briefly a member of The Nosebleeds with Morrissey, and one of the first to recognise the singer's potential.

73   Stipe's bandmates were guitarist Peter Buck, bassist Mike Mills and drummer Bill Berry.

74   Stipe and Morrissey are pictured together in Linder's *Morrissey Shot*, and 'Found, Found, Found' from *Kill Uncle* was rumoured to be about Stipe. In the case against Mike Joyce the judge notoriously described Morrissey as 'devious, truculent and unreliable', a phrase pounced on with glee by the music press. According to Morrissey, Stipe told him the judge was a 'fuckhead'.

By the time the solo Morrissey hit America in 1991, he was a star. Not in the sense of Whitney Houston or Mariah Carey, of course. There was no saturation media coverage, and his US chart positions make far from sensational reading. And yet, whenever Moz, Boz, Gaz and Spence rolled into town to play those legendary venues – Madison Square Gardens, the Hollywood Bowl, Roseland – an underground nation welled up in support and Mozmania held thousands in its thrall.

Waiting For The Man

Loretta Pasilias was born in October 1976 in Whittier, California, about 15 minutes from downtown Los Angeles. 'If you ever visit there,' she says, 'expect to see nothing but Mexican-Americans.' When she was ten years old her family moved to Pomona, a suburb of LA to the far east of the city. 'In Pomona,' she recalls, 'I was overwhelmed by all the African-Americans. It wasn't a big deal, just different.'

Loretta still lives in Pomona, but feels that it's something of a backwater. 'It takes me about 45 minutes going 80mph to get to Hollywood, where all the good stuff is. I do a lot of driving but I don't mind. Although I do plan on moving closer to LA once I graduate.'

Loretta remembers 1990 as the year that she discovered Morrissey, or 'The Man', as she sometimes refers to him. At the time she was in the eighth grade of junior high school, about 13 years old. Back then she listened to mainly rap music, like all of her friends. Rap appealed because her parents didn't approve of it, 'and I wanted to feel a bit rebellious.'

One day, two new girls arrived at the school who had a totally different style to the other kids, as well as a distinctly anglophile musical taste. The newcomers liked The Cure, The Smiths, Morrissey, Depeche Mode and New Order. At first she and her friends made fun of the new girls, but then, driven by curiosity, Loretta sampled some of their sounds for herself and found herself hooked.

'I never went so far as to wear Cure T-shirts and put patches all over my jackets and bags,' she says, 'but I did enjoy the music very much. I started buying cassettes. I believe the first one I bought was Kill Uncle when it came out. I memorised the lyrics to all the songs. I would write the lyrics to my favourite songs on my book covers. My room was filled with Morrissey posters.'

Moving up to high school, however, Loretta found her nascent Morrissey obsession was on the wane. 'I remember buying *Your Arsenal* and loving it,' she says, 'but I didn't go to any of those concerts, which I totally regret, because I think that was when Moz was at his best.'

Loretta graduated from high school in 1994 and started college at Claremont. At this point the Morrissey posters came down and she rarely listened to his music. But a mere three years later it started up again. In 1997, Morrissey rolled into town on the *Maladjusted* tour. When he walked onto the stage at Bridges Auditorium, Loretta was in the audience. 'It was the building where we had our high school graduation ceremony. This was my first Moz concert ever and I was so excited!' In the event, the performance zipped by so quickly that Loretta remembers almost no details of it. 'All I remember is it being too short and I was so sad at the end because it was over.'

After the show Loretta went out and bought all the Morrissey albums she had missed: *Beethoven Was Deaf, Vauxhall And I, Southpaw Grammar, World Of Morrissey* and *Maladjusted*. 'I was working at this trendy clothing store and I discovered that one of the chicks working with me was a Morrissey fan as well. Her name is Tracy. We became best Moz-friends.'

Together the duo have attended numerous concerts, conventions and signings. 'All the Oye! Esteban! concerts, every Moz event.' Tracy, now six months pregnant, is still keen to attend the next Morrissey convention in LA. 'We're making her a shirt that reads "Pregnant For The Last Time"', Loretta confides. 'I think she'll look cute in it.'[75]

75   The title of a 1991 Morrissey single.

'My friend, Dean,' Loretta continues, 'who lives five minutes from Morrissey, has a better chance of running into him than I do. Lots of people who live in that area run into him all the time – shopping, getting a haircut, at the post office. Lucky bastards!' Whenever Loretta visits Dean, she takes a small detour and drives up to Morrissey's house. His black BMW is almost always parked outside. 'I'll take a pic and send it to you.' she promises. 'I hope one day I'll get lucky and get to meet him as he's going out! And if I ever do I'll be sure to mention you!'

Daniel's story

Daniel Martinez is 17, and lives in California's San Fernando Valley, in the North Hills area above Los Angeles. He's been listening to The Smiths for two years, which, in the teenage scheme of things, seems like some considerable time. Although never really a big fan of what he terms 'Brit pop', Daniel did enjoy the '80s new wave music he occasionally heard at parties. 'At that time I was only into alternative rock,' he says, 'and some hip-hop, basically a lot of the mainstream stuff.'

During his sophomore year of High School, Daniel would hitch a ride to school with a friend called Steve.

> 'Usually he would have a Smiths or Morrissey tape. I never actually said anything. I didn't even listen to the music, I just kept quiet. Slowly, Steve started to tell me about this band and how his big sister got him into it, which surprised me because all my older siblings ever listened to was hip-hop.'

As his Sophomore year drew to an end, Daniel slowly found himself becoming more interested in The Smiths and their lead singer, Morrissey. Incredibly, at this point, Daniel hadn't listened to any of the lyrics at all,

> 'But the music sounded great to me, especially the guitar – I'm a fan of great guitar work. I asked Steve what albums he recommended, and he told me to just buy the two Best Of CDs, so I did.'[76]

Early that summer vacation, Daniel went to Las Vegas with his parents. He had forty dollars, and his first stop was the Virgin Megastore in Caesar's Palace. 'I bought the two CDs that would change the way I dressed, the way I thought, the way I danced, the two CDs that would change me – The Smiths, *Best...* and *Best II*' On the five-hour car journey home, he made his parents suffer by continually playing his new purchases.

> *'I immediately fell in love with "Bigmouth Strikes Again" and "This Charming Man". Of course, I couldn't really interpret them how they were meant to be, but they sounded great! At the time I was still into the mainstream stuff, but slowly becoming aware of other Brit pop bands like The Cure, Depeche Mode and New Order.'*

At the same time, another first love was entering Daniel's life. 'That same summer I started to become really close to an old friend from elementary school who I would soon ask to be my girlfriend. I asked out Marlene in mid-November of my junior year. I was so happy with her – she was the first girl who actually treated me right.'

But no Smiths fan would be complete without a healthy dose of emotional rejection. Daniel recalls bitterly:

> *'She dumped me five days before Christmas.'*[77] *'I was devastated. For two days straight I didn't eat, I had this sinking feeling all over my body. I finally stopped crying, and I listened to The Smiths. I slowly began to understand the music a lot more, and why Morrissey thinks that way about women.*[78] *Even though that sinking feeling was gone, I was very depressed, and began to think about what this*

---

76   An odd choice, since most hardcore Smiths fans deplore these annoyingly random compilations. A far better starting point would have been *The Queen Is Dead* or the *Hatful Of Hollow* and *The World Won't Listen* compilations.

77   Wonderfully appropriate for heartbroken soul-searching, 21 December is the longest night of the year.

78   Morrissey would no doubt point Daniel in the direction of the nearest feminist bookstore if he knew his young fan had detected an 'All women are bad' philosophy in his lyrics.

world and its people are REALLY like. I was literally spinning in circles, locked in my room realizing how much everything REALLY sucks! And this was all because of a few songs, Smiths songs!'[79]

Welcome to the World Of Morrissey, son. This way to debriefing. 'It took me a few months to realize how much I don't need to worry about these things.' Daniel continues, 'but by then I had already thrown away my junior year and a lot of friendships. I was still friends with Marlene and by the end of junior year, I dedicated "What Difference Does it Make?" directly to her, and she knew it. That break-up is what really got me into Morrissey's music, since then they [The Smiths] have been my favourite band ever!'

Final proof that Morrissey's music contains some kind of universal factor, providing the same kind of emotional crutch today for Hispanic boys in LA's hip-hop heartland as it did for English public schoolboys in the '80s.

'Even though I'm not as depressed as I used to be back then, I am able to understand the songs a lot better and enjoy them because of it. I am now a senior in high school, I grew a lot this past summer, mentally. I grew my own ideas and points of view, and Morrissey's poetry had a lot to do with their structure. Marlene and I worked out our differences that same summer, and we are once again dating, it's been eight months and I have dedicated "Interlude" to her.[80] So, as you can see, The Smiths and Moz have to do with a big part in my life, including my love life.'[81]

---

79   As a 19-year-old, I actually suffered similar symptoms after the end of an affair, and music did take on an extraordinarily powerful significance. One day, during this low ebb, my next door neighbour heard the sounds of Leonard Cohen coming from my house. She jumped over the garden fence, let herself in, ran up the stairs and burst into the room. 'No, Pat!' she warned. 'You must never listen to Leonard Cohen alone...'

80   Morrissey's 1994 duet with Siouxsie Sioux, a cover of a song by George de la Rue and Hal Shaper. Containing the line 'What seems like an interlude now could be the beginning of love', it failed to achieve the success of Nick Cave's similar pairing with Kylie Minogue on 'Where The Wild Roses Grow'.

81   'My Love Life' is a 1991 single by Morrissey, featuring Chrissie Hynde on backing vocals.

Far from becoming extinct, the Morrissey entity has strangely evolved in the land of Jennifer Lopez and Jerry Springer. I'm still not quite certain why, but the testimonies of thousands of fans seem to speak for themselves. Daniel concludes:

> 'I'm a big Smiths/Moz fan. I pretty much stopped listening to a lot of
> the mainstream music and now I listen to some Brit pop, punk, and recently
> underground hip-hop. Thanks to The Smiths, I can appreciate good lyrics,
> not just a beat.'

And the beat goes on. A different drum, for sure, but the Englishman with the quiff lurks behind it, a shadowy star of continuing cross-cultural significance.

Postscript: Loretta Meets The Man

E-mail dated 15 November 2000

HI PAT!!!!

I'm so happy! Still smiling.

Meeting Morrissey was just awesome. He did a signing for the release of his DVD, Oye! Esteban![82], here in Los Angeles at the Virgin Megastore on Sunset Boulevard (he also did one in New York). It took place last Monday at Midnight and 300 people got to meet him. I was one of the lucky ones. The previous Friday was when the wristbands for the event were given out at 9am.

There were to be no line-ups prior to 8am. Yeah, right. We got there at 11pm on Thursday. We camped out overnight – it was so fun. I went with my friend Tracy, who goes with me to every Moz event, and with these other three guys, friends of ours. We took plenty of alcohol and we got smashed. It was fun. There were also quite a few other friends of mine there – people who we know from concerts and

82   A US-only compilation.

conventions – and also a lot of people who chat on the Morrissey-solo website.[83]
I know a lot of people from there. I love being around all those Moz fans – it's great!

*We were searched before we entered the building. Then a girl asked for my name
and wrote it on a post-it note and attached it to the DVD (that's how he knew my
name). Then she handed me the DVD.*

*Pat, you won't believe how freaking nervous I was. It was so quiet inside, except for
some really mellow mood music playing in the background. Right before it was my
turn to go up, a security guy took all my things except for the DVD and told me
that I was not to touch Morrissey or take any pictures. Then I walked up to him.
He was wearing a beige jacket with like a blousey Morrissey-type shirt under-
neath. I didn't see his pants. His hair still looks good, thinning a little but not too
much. He looks great.*

*Anyway, I was so nervous when I actually walked up to that desk. I couldn't believe
I was face to face with him. It was very brief. I said, 'Hello, how are you?' and he
smiled and said, 'Hello, Loretta, how are you?' He said my name! I almost died. I
replied, 'Oh, a little cold from standing outside for so long.' Then he made a funny
face and grabbed my hand, and said, 'Oh', as if sympathizing with me. I couldn't
believe he was holding my hand, so I grabbed his with both of mine and held on!
Then his security people made me let go and that was it. It happened so, so fast.*

Controversy: Morrissey the racist?

In the '80s, Smiths and Morrissey fans tended to be white. Very white. In fact,
in those days, the average Morrissey fan was me: white, northern, middle-
class, educated, skinny, with weird hair and a million and one hang-ups about
virtually every aspect of life. Watch video footage of Morrissey's famous 1988
Wolverhampton concert, and you'll see what I mean.[84] There are a few non-
Caucasian faces among the kids lined up outside the Civic Hall, but in the

83   www.morrissey-solo.com is one of the best Morrissey websites.
84   Scenes from the concert were released as part of the *Hulmerist* compilation.

main the pastiness is blinding. I think this was one of the reasons why some music journalists had it in for The Smiths and Morrissey and were forever trying to smear them as somehow racist. In those days it was *de rigueur* for (white) music writers to rhapsodise about go-go, hip-hop, and the 'righteous anger of black America'.[85] Former *NME* Editor Danny Kelly, the man whose newshound instincts famously caused the demise of The Smiths in 1987, was a witness to the 'hip-hop wars' that divided the paper's staff in the late '80s. Half the staffers were evangelical hip-hop fans on a mission to educate their peers; the rest were into the quaint, shambling English indie music which more accurately reflected their reader's tastes.[86]

There were other anomalies. The annual readers' poll still included a category for 'Best reggae record', even though reggae had long ago ceased to be a vital force in the British music scene. And when the paper's critics voted for the greatest singles of all time in 1987 the incongruous winner was 'I Say A Little Prayer' by Aretha Franklin – certainly the definitive version of the Bacharach-David MOR classic, but a record and an artist that said precisely nothing about the *NME* and its readers at that time. Here, clearly, was a case of tokenism at its most pathetic.

But there's no doubt that Morrissey did make racially insensitive remarks during the '80s. 'All reggae is vile' can be defended as a statement of musical taste rather than of racial discrimination, and Morrissey was clearly taking his cue from ex-*NME* writers Tony Parsons and Julie Burchill.[87] As for his contemptuous remarks concerning Whitney Houston, again, these are to do with personal taste and witty nastiness rather than racism. But there was one comment which really stuck in the craw. When Morrissey said 'To get on *Top Of The Pops* you have to be black', he was clearly wrong.

---

85   Spearheaded by the band Trouble Funk, this '80s mutation of soul and funk was popular in Washington DC, but turned out to be a creative and commercial dead-end.

86   These artists became known as 'C-86 bands' after the *NME*'s C-86 compilation, featuring the jangly sounds of the early Primal Scream, among others.

87   Their book *The Boy Looked At Johnny* contained a chapter that attacked reggae for its misogyny, quasi-mysticism and musical conservatism.

IN THE IMAGE-CONSCIOUS EARLY '80S, MORRISSEY CUT AN EXCEPTIONALLY
CURIOUS FIGURE. THE FLOWERS WERE SAID TO BE HIS GESTURE OF DEFIANCE
AGAINST THE 'GREYNESS' OF THE TIMES.

Four

I Think I Can Help You Get Through Your Exams[88]

I would first have become aware of Morrissey around the autumn of 1983, when the second Smiths single, 'This Charming Man', entered the UK charts. At the time I was 14 years old and enjoying my first musical obsession – with the back catalogue of David Bowie. I didn't like the Smiths record and, in part, my dislike was informed by the fact that I didn't understand it.

It's strange, really, because I was quite a literary kid – certainly extremely pop-literate – and I'd painstakingly analysed every syllable of Bowie's '70s output. But The Smiths were odd and different, and something about 'This Charming Man' plunged me into a state of bewilderment and smouldering semi-outrage. I decided that The Smiths were rubbish. And yet they fascinated me. A lot of people took an instant, instinctive dislike to The Smiths, so I was far from alone in this gut reaction. Writer and comedian Sean Hughes was slagging the band off to his friends before he'd even properly heard them: 'I think I was in love with them even then.' he said, years later. I know what he means.

On the face of it, The Smiths were just another cheerfully scruffy jangly guitar group of the time, like Aztec Camera, early Orange Juice, The Bluebells, or even The Icicle Works. But Morrissey's lyrics to 'This Charming Man', which I read in either *Smash Hits* or *Number One*, were what truly set them apart. There was definitely method here, in the coded references I later realised came from such sources as Anthony Shaeffer's *Sleuth* ('You're nothing but a jumped-up pantry boy who doesn't know his place!'), but there was also an

88   From 'Handsome Devil'.

element of the outsider artist about Morrissey.[89] In his early pictures, before he became an icon, I always thought he looked a bit simple, like a doltish, idiot savant farmhand who carries a chicken everywhere, but might just save you from losing a limb in a combine harvester.

When I started reading *Smash Hits* in 1982, it covered a lot of fairly grown-up pop music. The Jam, Japan, The Teardrop Explodes, Bauhaus and many others all made the cover. By 1983, however, the molten lava from the new pop eruption had cooled and solidified; the cover of *Smash Hits* was now ruled by more conservative acts like the Eurythmics or teenybopper outfits such as Kajagoogoo.

No matter what the serious critics said at the time, however, the early '80s was a very interesting period for pop music. As a young teenager, though, I couldn't help feeling that I'd turned on to the whole thing just as it was reaching its peak, in 1982. By the following year I could tell that something had died – the life had drained from this colourful and glorious post-punk canvas. And by 1985 virtually the entire UK music scene had stagnated. It did pick up, of course, and there was a steady flow of exciting moments for the next decade or so: from The Jesus And Mary Chain to 'Pump Up The Volume', from Suede to Pulp, from Madchester to Britpop.[90] One may be hard pushed to name a single convincing British band in 2003, but surely the next renaissance must be close at hand.

A Chance To Shine[91]

Between 1981 and 1986, there were many post-punk groups with odd hair scoring one-off hits and appearing on Top Of The Pops. There were The Pinkees with 'Danger Games' and Blue Zoo with 'Cry Boy Cry'. A bit later

89   In the film of the play these words are spat at a cowering Michael Caine by Laurence Olivier.
90   The Jesus and Mary Chain were serious rivals to The Smiths between 1985 and 1987. Jim and William Reid's band specialised in sweetly-twisted pop songs backed with howling guitar feedback. 'Pump Up The Volume', the pioneering dance track by MARRS, was a UK number one in September 1987.
91   The title of a Morrissey fanzine, taken from 'Sing Your Life'.

came Re-Flex with 'The Politics Of Dancing', H2O with 'I Dream To Sleep' and Fiction Factory with '(Feels Like) Heaven'. Some of these tracks would appear alongside The Smiths' 'What Difference Does It Make' on the best-selling *Now That's What I Call Music Volume 2* compilation album in early 1984. The Smiths, however, outdistanced the field. They scored hit after hit in the UK – from the soaringly lugubrious 'Heaven Knows I'm Miserable Now' in 1984 to the oddly touching 'Girlfriend In A Coma' at the end of 1986, they impacted on the national pop consciousness far more than any of their rivals. Admittedly their records received little radio airplay, and many of the singles charted no higher than number 24 (the relatively weak 'Shakespeare's Sister') or 47 (a disappointing showing for the masterful 'That Joke Isn't Funny Any More'), but more than any of their rivals, The Smiths kept them coming. The singles flew thick and fast – four or five a year, and the albums weren't far behind. Like The Beatles or The Rolling Stones or Bob Dylan in the '60s, The Smiths gave the impression of being a dynamic creative unit who were flying towards the peak of their powers. Their entry in *The Guinness Book Of British Hit Singles* is impressive, not least because it contains the most amusing collection of song titles of any group or artist ever. In their short existence, The Smiths certainly made their mark. By 1984 they had usurped the place held by Echo And The Bunnymen as the hippest group in Britain, and therefore the world. To be fair, cult rivals The Cure were probably a bit bigger than The Smiths at this time, but they somehow never inspired the same critical reverence.

Of course, the really big acts of the year were Wham! (two number ones and a number two, plus a solo chart-topper for singer George Michael) and the Liverpool phenomenon Frankie Goes To Hollywood (three number ones and total chart dominance), but everyone knew that, unlike the already-imploding Frankie, The Smiths had the equipment necessary to stay the distance.

The last couple of Smiths singles, indifferently culled from *Strangeways Here We Come* in 1987, blotted the copybook slightly. With hints of both glam and rockabilly, not to mention a smidgeon of soul, 'I Started Something I Couldn't Finish' was a great album track, but hardly destined to trouble the hated (well, hated by Morrissey anyway) 'Do They Know It's Christmas?' in the all-time best-seller stakes. At the time, 'Last Night I Dreamt That Somebody Loved Me' seemed like a compendium of Smiths clichés compacted into three miserable minutes. In retrospect, it's a mini-masterpiece, but this was the year of 'Pump Up The Volume' and the beginnings of the ecstasy-fuelled dance music revolution. With the demise of The Smiths themselves, Rough Trade struggled to bring their swansong to the masses.

Keats and Yeats are on your side[92]

I successfully resisted The Smiths for a good four years until the late summer of 1987. I moved into my first student house in Oxford a week or so before my fellow occupants and, after a few days, found myself feeling depressed. There was a Smiths tape lying around in one of the rooms and I started to listen to it. The first song was 'London', a blast of adrenal punk far harder, harsher and more vehement than I'd supposed The Smiths were capable of. 'Unlovable' was a gorgeous pop song even though Morrissey sang it like a man utterly bereft of hope ('I don't have much in my life, but take it, it's yours'), while 'Rubber Ring' was a skanking gem, with a tight, funky groove and a uniquely impassioned lyric about how old songs are a boy's best friend, although the scary voice at the end repeating the words, 'You are sleeping, you do not want to believe' gave me the creeps.[93] If I wasn't exactly suicidal when I started listening to The Smiths, I was by the time I'd heard 'Asleep'.[94] I wasn't alone. All over the world serious boys were feeling its icy fingers trail up and down their slender spines at dangerous hours of the night.

92   From 'Cemetry Gates'.
93   Supposedly culled from a recording of 'voices of the dead' on a flexidisc given away with paranormal magazine *The Unexplained*. The accompanying feature in the magazine suggested that celebrated inventor Thomas Edison had initially conceived the phonograph as a means of communicating with the dead. Instead, he accidentally gave birth to the recording industry and thereby ultimately provided Morrissey with a career.
94   It seems strange to admit it, but I avoided 'Asleep'. I truly believed it could inspire suicidal feelings, and I still skip over it today.

It was a good thing that I'd belatedly become a Smiths fan, because I'd been an avid reader of the *NME* for over a year, and Smiths knowledge was highly necessary to an understanding of a large percentage of that paper's headers, sell-lines and captions.[95] I'd started reading the *NME* in the spring of 1986, attracted by its nostalgic coverage of the tenth anniversary of punk. A free vinyl EP attached to the front cover contained 'Some Candy Talking' by The Jesus And Mary Chain and 'Downtown Train' by Tom Waits, as well as a live version of The Beatles' 'Ticket To Ride' performed by Husker Du.[96] The tales of punk excited me far more than anything then happening in the UK music scene, and I got heavily into the Sex Pistols, The Clash and The Stranglers, while also doing my research into The Buzzcocks, Sham 69 and Richard Hell And The Voidoids. I sent off for an *NME* compilation tape called *Pogo-a-go-go*, which contained tracks by everyone from The Pistols and The Damned to Alternative TV, The Television Personalities and Shane MacGowan's Nipple Erectors. I later learned that The Manic Street Preachers had also had their musical imaginations fired by the same music at the same time and via the same catalyst of the *NME*. The charts that summer were dominated by the conveyor-belt pop of Stock, Aitken And Waterman and pop-rock hits such as the Doctor And The Medics version of 'Spirit In The Sky, 'Addicted To Love' by Robert Palmer and 'Money For Nothing' by Dire Straits. All classics in their way, but there was something lumbering and graceless then about even the best mainstream product. There had to be more to life.

I lost interest in the *NME* for a bit, because it featured hopeless-looking bands with stupid names that I'd never heard of; and therefore I missed out on the paper's coverage of *The Queen Is Dead*, which I later realised to have been one of the musical events of the '80s. A few months later I was at Oxford and getting into indie music, and my college's Junior Common Room had a subscription to the *NME*.

And so, the following year, I moved into that house off the Cowley Road and discovered The Smiths. And a few weeks later they split up.

---

95 'That Joke Isn't Funny Any More' and 'William, It Was Really Nothing' being particularly popular sources of wordplay.

96 US hardcore punk band fronted by Bob Mould and seen as forerunners of grunge.

In retrospect, the spirit of Morrissey was a very real presence at Oxford in the late '80s.[97] On my way to John Carey's lecture on Milton ('In *Paradise Lost*,' he memorably asserted, 'God not only has a personality, he also has personality problems'.) I encountered another English student I knew slightly. He was toting a copy of a Smiths album, I can't remember which one. Someone had played him 'Cemetery Gates', with its references to Keats, Yeats and Wilde and its themes of plagiarism and literary one-upmanship. The song had amused him, so he'd gone out and bought this album which unfortunately did not contain it. He didn't like any of the other songs, so he was hanging around where English students congregated, trying to sell it.

The Smiths were on their way to being ancient history by the time of the sweltering summer of 1989 (my trendy young friends in the first year had already trooped up to the Poly to experience their generational epiphany in the form of The Stone Roses), but I remember hearing about this first year kid lying out on the quad in the heat of the day, dressed head to toe in black. When someone asked him if he wasn't a little hot he replied, 'I wear black on the outside because that is how I feel on the inside', a line from 'Unlovable'.[98] I thought it was quite a cool and funny thing to say, although this same kid also reckoned that David Bowie's *Never Let Me Down* was a great album.[99]

Do you think you made the right decision this time?[100]

In 1990 I moved to London and got a job working for French Railways, the SNCF. I was a highly incompetent ticketing clerk based in the SNCF office in Piccadilly, opposite the Royal Academy Of Arts. I did not prosper there, and on one ignominious occasion I issued an incomplete ticket which left 500 Lourdes-bound pilgrims stranded on a station platform somewhere in

97   Certainly, the Oxford HMV shop stocked more Smiths T-shirts than for any other band or artist.

98   As a matter of fact, Morrissey appears to have no particular fondness for black clothes.

99   This album is generally considered Bowie's worst.

100   From 'London'.

Switzerland. My one friend in the office, apart from some of the sexy French girls (Morrissey would never have approved of these femmes fatales, who appeared to wear fur coats and leather trousers in all weathers), was aspiring comedy writer Hugh Rycroft, who later supplied gags to everyone from Mel And Sue to Jerry Springer. Hugh was a big Smiths fan. He played me a bootleg tape of The Smiths performing at the Oxford Apollo in 1985. He had a recording of Morrissey and Howard Devoto camping it up on Janice Long's Radio 1 show in 1987. ('If I was Samantha Fox's manager,' quoth Morrissey, rolling his Rs like Lady Bracknell, 'I would put her in a very big box and send her to the Shetland Islands.') We would sit around Hugh's trash-strewn ground-floor flat opposite Hippo Pizza in Tooting Broadway and analyse tracks like 'I Keep Mine Hidden' ('He's referring to his emotions.' Hugh opined, with scholarly gravitas. 'His genitals, surely.' I quipped, a pseudo-baggy Evelyn Waugh wannabe.) and 'Girl Least Likely To', where Morrissey's impressively callous disembowelment of an aspiring yet hapless writer made us shift uncomfortably on Hugh's collapsing sofa ('There's a publisher, she says, in the new year,' sneered the man. 'It's never in this year.').

In the SNCF building there was a small and airless subterranean room where members of staff were permitted to eat their lunch. I never used it much, mainly because I disliked a certain group of people who tended to congregate there. I am not very interested in politics, but I privately referred to this cadre as 'the moaning Tories', because they always used to go on about how much they hated everything. On one occasion I overheard a conversation that went something like this:

> 'Did you see that Julian Clary on TV last night?' 'God, I hate him!' 'You know, Hitler put people like him in camps, and I think he might have had the right idea.'

I'm not making this up; it really was as ugly and stupid and nasty and wrong as that. I felt strangely protective of Clary, whose piano player Russell Churney had been a well-liked Head Boy at my school (Russell's sister Sophie later sang with Liverpool indie band Ooberman). I didn't say anything, but from then on I made it known in the office that I spent much of my free time getting stoned with the gay man who lived in the flat above mine, and that I was a frequenter of homosexual dance music clubs.

Sometime that August I was walking along Piccadilly after work when I saw a flyposter for a magazine called *Outlook*. Two weeks later I left the SNCF and started work on *Outlook* as its unpaid Music Editor. A year on, I put together a Morrissey feature for the magazine, including interviews with Stephen Street and Sandie Shaw, and contributions from writers as diverse as Hugh Rycroft and Mark Simpson. The Morrissey issue went on to be the biggest seller *Outlook* ever had, and it gave Philip Garner, one of the magazine's designers, the notion of launching a pop culture publishing venture named The Dunce Directive. His first product took the form of my 6,000 word essay *Bigmouth: Morrissey 1983-1993*.[101]

It was in 1991 that I finally got to see Morrissey play live for the first time. On a grey night that July he attempted an uncharacteristically muscle-flexing show of strength by playing at Wembley Arena, a resolutely atmosphere-free shed next to the famous north London football stadium and opposite the site of the old Empire Pool, where Morrissey icons like Bowie and Bolan enthralled the masses two decades earlier. Despite claims that the gig was sold out, the venue was not full, but there were an awful lot of people there, and there was a sense of jubilation in the air. *Kill Uncle* was out, and, as it had not yet been decreed one of the all-time turkeys, most of us liked at least some of the tracks. Images of Morrissey culled from the album's cover art could be seen all over London – in record shop windows, on billboards, on the cover of *Time Out*. There he was, his eyes imploring, his arms outstretched, his quiff straining towards Heaven. I remember saying to Hugh Rycroft, only half-jokingly, 'These are our people'. When the band came on (somehow I managed to miss Phranc, the lesbian folk-singer support act, although I quite liked her records), I could not help but sing along to every song.

In August 1992 I got a call from one of the editors of *Lime Lizard* magazine, a highly likable loon named Patrick (his partner Britt Collins was soon to win

---

101 'Tediously written dung', according to the *NME*. Rather more gratifyingly, I have
     encountered numerous Morrissey fans who enjoyed the book, and it continues to sell
     around the world.

notoriety after receiving death threats from Kurt Cobain and Courtney Love).
He wanted me to attend the launch party for Morrissey's new album, *Your
Arsenal*, which was taking place that evening. The catch was that I was
expected to then hop on a tube to the *Lime Lizard* offices in Highbury &
Islington and bash out a review of the album – or rather a newsy preview –
before the magazine went to press the next day.

Things had not been going well for me. I'd been on the dole for almost two
years and was nowhere near to earning a living as a journalist. I'd left *Outlook*
after arguments over the editorial direction, and I was missing the surrogate
family provided by its rag-tag assortment of music freaks, Eco-fascists, hippy
activists, terminally paranoid cannabis legalisation types and young, ambitious
writers.[102] I also missed the invitations it received to numerous events where
the presence of free food was the main attraction for a lean and hungry
would-be hack. As I roused myself from a depressive fug that Morrissey
himself would have been proud of, I almost returned to my West Dulwich
bed when I realised I had no clean socks (in this respect I was rather like
Orwell, I fancy, who, though starving to death, threw away a pan of milk
when a fly plopped into it).

The *Your Arsenal* launch party was held at a small club off Regent Street, on
the far western perimeter of Soho.[103] Music journalists, some quite famous, all
of them more successful than me, were laughing loudly at music journalist
jokes and attacking the free beer. Skint as always, I was pathetically grateful
when I realised I didn't have to pay for my drinks. Gary Day and Boz Boorer
wandered by. Paralysed with shyness, I didn't even consider the possibility of
grabbing them for a quote. Instead, I stood by myself and listened to the
album, which was played at least twice that night. The affable Murray

---

102   Matt Arnoldi and Pete Fruin – two music freaks in particular who were great talent
      scouts, and on whose recommendation I commissioned the first ever published
      interview with Suede.
103   The title of the album combines a mention of the famous north-London football team
      Arsenal (celebrated in Nick Hornby's *Fever Pitch*) with the implication of the combative
      phrase 'Up your arse'. In this it recalls the punning title of John Lahr's biography of Joe
      Orton, *Prick Up Your Ears*, made into a film starring Gary Oldman in 1987.

Chalmers, then Morrissey's press officer (now working with the Pet Shop Boys and Kylie Minogue), saw me taking notes, and came over. 'The first track sounds amazing.' I gushed, referring to the fiery 'You're Gonna Need Someone On Your Side'. 'Yeah,' he enthused, 'it sounds like The Cramps!'[104]

The album certainly rocked, and managed to translate a shameless Bowie influence ('Glamorous Glue' borrowed from 'Gene Genie', 'The National Front Disco' from 'Absolute Beginners', and the glorious penultimate track 'I Know It's Gonna Happen Some Day' owed more than a little to 'Rock 'n' roll Suicide') into something new, vital and essentially Morrissey-like. I knew it had to mark an upturn in Morrissey's fortunes after the mauling of *Kill Uncle*. On the other hand, I couldn't help noticing that it wasn't a very happening party. Although the special edition 78 rpm ten-inch single of 'You're The One For Me, Fatty' with which we were issued caused a ripple of excitement, there was a palpable sense of disappointment with the fact that there was no sign of Morrissey himself. The free record came in a white plastic bag which bore on one side the '60s logo of Parlophone Records, and on the other the corresponding logo for Capitol. I've always wondered what Morrissey meant by this (if indeed his control freakery did extend to the printing of special plastic bags for this occasion alone). I think that in a way he was stating — consciously or unconsciously — that Britain and the USA may contentedly coexist in record collections, where The Beatles and The Beach Boys snuggle together, but that they remain two separate universes; as incomparably unalike as Wolverhampton Civic Hall and the Hollywood Bowl. Taking into account the wilfully archaic format of the freebie record, it seemed to me that Morrissey was also saying, 'The past is another country, they do things differently there — and that is where I belong'.

The Stretford Warhol

If nothing else, Steven Patrick Morrissey would have been remembered as the greatest record sleeve designer of the '80s. Indeed, the best book yet published

---

104   Cult US psychobilly band, reviewed by Morrissey for *Record Mirror* in the late '70s.

on pop's prime enigma is not Johnny Rogan's exhaustive and exhausting 500-pager *Morrissey And Marr: The Severed Alliance*, but a picture book of Smiths and Morrissey solo sleeve designs entitled *Peepholism* and compiled by the singer's longtime collaborator, the designer Jo Slee. While no one can deny that Rogan did his spadework, the major achievement of *The Severed Alliance* is to depict The Smiths as the most boring band in the history of rock music. Peepholism is much more interesting. While tacitly endorsed by the man himself, Jo Slee's commentary on the sleeves of those singles and albums is witty, perceptive and surprisingly revealing. Her turn of phrase is engagingly Morriseyesque to the extent that one might almost suspect that it was the work of Morrissey himself. It's weird, though, that while Rogan devoted years of his life to interviewing Morrissey's family, music business colleagues, even kids who vaguely remembered him from primary school, the reader still comes away knowing virtually nothing about him. Jo Slee, on the other hand, experienced Morrissey's creative process at first hand and probably knows as much about it as any of his songwriting partners, with the possible exception of Johnny Marr. Working with Morrissey was clearly a rewarding experience for Slee, who delights in documenting his preference for obscure typefaces and highly specific colours. Most crucially of all, though, is the singer's choice of subject matter, for the Smiths record sleeves almost always featured images of people who held some significance for Morrissey. This could be confusing to non-Smiths fans. In 1987 the 'Shoplifters Of The World Unite' single carried an image of Elvis Presley on the sleeve, making it look to the casual punter like an Elvis record. And when Northen eccentric Viv Nicholson, of *Spend! Spend! Spend!* fame, appeared on the cover of 'Heaven Knows I'm Miserable Now' in 1984, some people thought it was actually Moors Murderer Myra Hindley.[105] For each sleeve, negotiations had to be undertaken to secure the right to use these images; *Peepholism* recounts such instances. Terrence Stamp refused permission for The Smiths to use a still from *The Collector*, but later relented. Albert Finney, another key figure of '60s British cinema, never gave his consent and so missed out on his place in Smiths iconography. Despite the provincially-flavoured British bias,

---

105 Both women modelled the peroxide beehive hairstyle that enjoyed near-ubiquity in the north during the mid-'60s.

there was something quite Warholian in Morrissey's magpie-eyed appropriation of other people's charisma. Appropriately enough, the cover of the first Smiths album features a still from a Warhol film entitled *Flesh*.[106] As *Peepholism* reveals, however, the sleeve image has been cropped, and the original still is a voyeuristic glimpse of two men sharing a casually intimate moment. This kind of thing happens a lot with Morrissey: in-jokes, obscure references, coded slang, the suggestion of secret knowledge. The harder you look at the picture, the more you realise you don't have a clue what's really going on.

Meet the Ex-Smiths

Mike Joyce

Mike Joyce doesn't walk; he charges, thundering up and down the stairs of his well-appointed Cheshire home, tilting at windmills both real and imaginary. Usually and accurately described as bluff, he is disarmingly open, even when he's trying to be guarded, which is not often. Having spent almost a third of his life in litigation, he has had to cultivate an almost superhuman patience.[107] Now that the case is over and he has won, he is making up for lost time, doing everything at five times the average speed, like Morrissey's Spring-Heel Jim.[108] For some time he has been considering writing a book about his experiences, either as sole author or in collaboration with Andy Rourke, to whom he remains close.

---

106   As Morrissey would have been aware, despite appearing under the Warhol banner, *Flesh* was actually the work of Warhol associate Paul Morrissey.

107   After the dissolution of The Smiths, Andy Rourke and Mike Joyce discovered that in legal terms they had never been Smiths at all – the band was effectively Morrissey and Marr. The rhythm section alleged that they were owed various monies dating from their time with the band, and pursued their former bandmates through the courts for several years. Rourke accepted an out-of-court settlement, said to be £60,000. Joyce continued with his case and was eventually awarded a much more substantial sum. Producer Stephen Street and Craig Gannon, who was briefly a member of The Smiths, have also fought legal actions against Morrissey.

108   From *Vauxhall And I*.

I encounter him when he and Andy are invited to judge a band competition at London's Mean Fiddler in November 2000. 'I think now's the time to talk about it,' he says in an uncharacteristically serious tone, 'instead of arguing about who bought a hot dog for who in 1984.'

He always reminds me of a boxer (something else Morrissey has sung about); a plucky Irish scrapper. There's a good black and white picture of him from years ago, posing with bare knuckles ready for action. He could knock your block off, could Mike Joyce.

Earlier, in 1999, I visit Mike at his home to interview him for *Rhythm* magazine. He's full of energy and high spirits, showing me the cellar that he's converted into a music room. The walls are adorned with gold and silver discs for Smiths albums sales, and there's a Yamaha drum kit set up and ready to go. He urges me to try it out, but I decline, citing musical incompetence. I'm a lousy drummer. Instead, Mike plugs in a cheap Danelectro reissue guitar belonging to Aziz Ibrahim, the guitarist who replaced John Squire in The Stone Roses, and hands it to me. I strum a few chords and Mike attacks his drums. It becomes apparent that he is an excellent rock drummer, laying down fat, heavy grooves punctuated with succinct, punchy fills. I have a hard time keeping up with his metronomic beat, and the cheap, sharp strings of the Danelectro hurt my fingertips. It's great fun, though. This has all the makings of a proud musical moment, if only I could remember some of Johnny Marr's notoriously tricky chord sequences. I unplug the guitar and ask Mike to play some of my favourite drum tracks from Smiths songs – the cascading toms at the end of 'That Joke Isn't Funny Any More', the machine gun snare break from 'The Queen Is Dead', the pulsing groove of 'How Soon Is Now?'. It's a measure of how great these records were that just hearing their unadorned drum tracks is enough to set my pulse racing.

Mike scoops a handful of cassettes from a shoebox; recordings of rehearsals from the earliest days of The Smiths back in 1982. We listen to them on a battered old tape player in the kitchen, and Mike has to hold the tape in with his finger while it plays. It's amazing stuff: the infant band sounds tight and assured, Morrissey sings in a much lower register ('Mogadon rock' quips

Mike), and there are different arrangements of songs with added instruments like keyboards and trumpets. There's a famous story about the time when the musicians who would later become world famous as Led Zeppelin first got together.[109] Jimmy Page, Robert Plant, John Paul Jones and John Bonham assembled in a room, elected to play 'Train Kept A-rolling', someone counted them in, and a huge noise erupted, engulfing the musicians like the mushroom cloud from a nuclear blast. They looked at one another and knew they had a sound that would conquer the world. When you listen to those early tapes of 'Handsome Devil' and 'Reel Around The Fountain' it is apparent that something similar, although immeasurably more subtle, feminine and subversive, was taking place in that Manchester rehearsal space in 1982. When you hear a great band, it just hits you in the heart.

Andy Rourke

He's put on a bit of weight in the last year or two, but former Smiths bassist Andy Rourke retains the moptopped image of scuffed cool that is a requisite for Mancunian pop stars living and dead. Hopping into a London black cab outside a hotel in Victoria, he asks the driver to take us to The Mean Fiddler in Harlesden. The driver doesn't know where Harlesden is. 'Haven't you done the knowledge, mate?' Rourke asks, irritated. The driver turns nasty – very nasty, in fact – and orders us out of his cab. Rourke informs him that he can go fuck himself. We get another cab. As the taxi ride unfolds like a Suede song, Andy's annoyance recedes. He points to a showroom full of luxury cars with a name I've never heard before. 'Liam had one of those.' he says. 'I think Patsy made him get rid of it.'[110]

Andy's own girlfriend – young, blonde, very pretty, very ambitious – starts telling a story. 'We were on the train back from London and it was full of Man U supporters, so the conductor moved us into first class. Some of the fans came in. They weren't nasty or anything, but they started taking the piss,

109   Never a critics' favourite, Led Zeppelin are the second most successful band of all time after The Beatles, a feat achieved despite their policy of never releasing singles.
110   Liam Gallagher and Patsy Kensit.

calling him John Lennon because of the hair and the shades.'

'And then,' Andy continues, 'they started calling me Johnny Marr, which was a bit strange. I thought, "If only you knew".'

The cab streaks west towards Queens Park and beyond. Rourke recognises the area. 'When The Smiths moved to London in 1984, Morrissey had a massive flat in Kensington and Johnny had a nice place in Earls Court,' he remembers, 'and Mike and I shared a flat round here.' He winces at the grubbiness of the memory. 'It was a shithole.' he says.

I remember an incident in the early '90s when I was back in Liverpool. I was mooching around the trendy new shops tacked on to the side of the Baa Bar (the city's answer to Manchester's infamous Dry), when I suddenly noticed that a silver disc for *Strangeways Here We Come* was affixed to the wall in the café I'd strolled into. It had Andy Rourke's name on it, and I surmised that the bassist must have been forced to sell the item during a spell of post-Smiths penury. I stood there looking at it, feeling depressed. A month later, I was back in Liverpool and I returned to the café, intent on stealing the disc and maybe even returning it one day to its former owner. Needless to say, it was no longer there.[111]

Johnny Marr: the significant other

And what has become of Morrissey's one-time partner and creative equal, Johnny Marr? Sadly, the answer seems to be that the man who everybody said Morrissey would be nothing without has spent the past 14 years doing a pretty good job of being nothing himself. What a waste. The title of Johnny Rogan's famous book, *Morrissey And Marr: The Severed Alliance*, is somewhat misleading – it's essentially a Morrissey biography with a few references to the tousle-fringed guitarist – but it does accurately reflect the esteem in which Marr was

---

111   I last saw Andy at V2001 in Stafford during Coldplay's set. He was heading to the bar with the air of a man who goes to check out the 'new Smiths' every few years and is always – understandably – underwhelmed.

held. Music Journalist Michael Leonard told me about Smiths-centric conversations in which he and an old friend had indulged on many a late-night drinking session. 'We used to try and work out which songs were basically Morrissey saying "I love you" to Marr,' Michael said, with a wry smile, 'and we came to the conclusion that it was pretty much all of them.' And, you know, he's got a point.

Skip now to 'I Won't Share You', the unbelievably plaintive closing track on the final Smiths album (*Strangeways Here We Come*, 1987); lend an ear to 'I Keep Mine Hidden', the last thing the band ever recorded. Once you get into your head the rogue notion that this is a love letter from Morrissey to Johnny, it becomes difficult to shake. Consider 'Please Please Please Let Me Get What I Want' – one hundred seconds of naked emotion delivered from the lyricist to his musician; a confession of Morrissey's secret dreams intended for Johnny's ears only that somehow became the property of the whole world. Even from my own limited experiences as an amateur musician, I know full well that being in a band is a very strange experience psychologically. You do things to each other's minds that you simply wouldn't do if you were merely friends. And writing a song with somebody is more intimate than sex; you're giving your co-creators access to parts of your psyche that you would never dream of revealing to anyone else. Okay, maybe the songwriting process isn't like that for, say, Limp Bizkit, but I'm pretty sure it was for Morrissey and Marr. Songwriting of that order is a communion of minds. In their shabby bedrooms and damp rehearsal rooms, whenever they went into a huddle to work out some new idea (quickly, of course; for these boys always worked quickly), Morrissey and Johnny were, for those fast-burning seconds of the creative process, more closely tied together than the most devoted married couple.

Johnny Marr was a down-to-earth youngster. He carried his talent like one of his beloved Rickenbacker guitars – casually, and yet with full awareness of its power. And yet, since the day he split up The Smiths in 1987 (he told *Mojo* in 2001 that it was because he could no longer tolerate Morrissey's control freakery), he has produced precisely nothing which survives comparison with his prodigious musical output during those five short years.

Examining the musical projects Marr undertook towards the end of The Smiths and shortly afterwards is a depressing experience. He fails to breathe much life into the once mighty talents of Bryan Ferry and Talking Heads. The albums he made with The The are more satisfying, but these are very much Matt Johnson's show, and Johnson — himself a capable musician and producer, and a formidable songwriter — seems unable to allow Marr to express himself freely. Admittedly, in interviews Johnson denies this, taking pains to praise Marr in both personal and professional terms, and insisting that he was a full member of The The. But still, this is very much not the impression you get when listening to 1989's *Mind Bomb* and 1992's *Dusk*.

Electronic, Marr's post-Smiths collaboration with New Order's Bernard Sumner, was, however, a commercial success. A Madchester supergroup with musical credibility to burn, Electronic produced two glossy, appealing hit singles in 'Getting Away With It' (1989) and 'Get The Message' (1990). Their debut album, *Electronic*, was a major success in 1990, but is a curiously empty listening experience, and is not now remembered as a classic. Electronic have continued to record sporadically, but with ever-diminishing returns, while Johnny's own band The Healers came and went with barely a murmur. His one great moment in recent years came in 2000 when, appearing at a concert in honour of the late Linda McCartney, he performed a stunning version of 'Meat Is Murder', carrying off the lead vocal with verve and courage.[112] The old magic, it was clear, was not dead; merely dormant.[113]

112   He was introduced onstage by Chrissie Hynde of The Pretenders, herself a notable animal rights activist, who has also worked with Morrissey.
113   Marr also played a part in the rise of Oasis, Britain's biggest band of the '90s. In 2002 he contributed guitar tracks to the latest Oasis album, *Heathen Chemistry*.

THE SMITHS TOWARDS THE END:
(LEFT TO RIGHT) MIKE JOYCE, ANDY ROURKE, MORRISSEY, JOHNNY MARR

Five

With Your Mascara And Your Fender Guitar[114]

On a freezing cold day in the first month of 2000, I arrive at an ugly industrial estate in Mill Hill, a place where part of the original walls of old London Town meet the open countryside. I find a tiny shack which is a music shop, and I'm pleased to see that it sells *Rhythm*, the specialist drum magazine which I'm working for, along with sister titles like *Guitarist*, *Bassist* and *Total Guitar*. The man behind the counter directs me to a shabby rehearsal room, from which I can hear the sounds of 'Shoplifters Of The World Unite'.

I slip inside and sit shivering on an old sofa as Morrissey's band run through their set. Boz, Alain, Spike and Gary all look the part, accoutred in rockabilly regalia. The uniform runs to brothel creepers, black shirts adorned with yellow flames and red devils, and vintage jeans with the kind of turn-ups that everyone else stopped wearing around the time Bros appropriated the look in 1988.[115] They're a tight little unit, playing the songs through, making tweaks and revisions, tempo changes. Occasionally, as on 'Shoplifters Of The World Unite', Alain will take a lead vocal, revealing a fine singing voice, heartfelt and yearning. On the floor Alain has a CD case containing just about every song Morrissey has ever recorded. Their leader might at any time request new additions to the set, requiring the band to all learn a song that none of them has ever played live before. This has been a common occurrence recently, with Morrissey seemingly gripped with the urge to sing old Smiths numbers again.

114 From 'Get Off The Stage'.
115 A briefly-successful UK pop trio managed by svengali Tom Watkins and featuring blonde twins Matt and Luke Goss.

Like commandos awaiting sealed orders, the band are still unsure of where the forthcoming tour will take them. They just know they have to be ready. And so they rehearse in the Mill Hill chill, while Morrissey languishes under the Hollywood sun in the house built by Clark Gable. In the event, the tour will turn out to be one of their biggest and most successful ever, with the band traversing almost the entire length of both North and South America, from Seattle near the top to Santiago near the bottom.[116] Needless to say, its magnitude barely registers in Britain.

I observe the band. The guitarist and musical director Boz Boorer is tall, slightly imposing and seemingly rather reserved. Although he has gained a few pounds and grey hairs in the last few years, he carries that dignified quality that you get with older rockers.

Alain Whyte, who looks handsome and boyish in photos, is disarmingly friendly, a vibey guy, who has been a handy talent-spotter for Morrissey over the years, roping in appropriate musicians from his forays into the underbelly of the London music scene. That's how he found Anglesey-born drummer Spike T Smith, a thoroughly solid bloke, who nailed his colours to the mast of punk rock in his boyhood. I first met Spike in 1999 when he was drumming with punk stalwarts The Damned, filling the seat vacated by his boyhood hero Rat Scabies. We hooked up at a gig in Bristol where The Damned played an excellent set that successfully blended the punk, goth and psychedelia of their various incarnations. Guitarist Captain Sensible was back in the line-up and bassist Patricia Morrison from the Sisters Of Mercy was also on board. It seemed like a good occasion to get drunk and go dancing at the Bierkeller, where a weird thing happened. After playing the usual late '90s indie disco fare to a near-empty house, the DJ suddenly tired of Blur's 'Song 2' and Green Day's 'Basket Case' and slipped 'Panic' by The Smiths into the playlist.[117] I took the opportunity to dance like a fool, the only other people on the dancefloor being a near-comatose businessman and the tall, impossibly leggy, and feasibly transvestite prostitute he'd somehow ended up with. I remember she gyrated like a pole-dancing Cindy Crawford and

116   The tour is recorded in the unofficially-released *South With Morrissey* DVD.
117   'Panic' is infamous for its supposedly inflammatory 'Hang the DJ' refrain.

seemed to know the words. 'Bit of a Smiths fan, are you, eh?' Spike asked when I plonked down, giddy and sweating.

I was also drunk when I bumped into Spike at that year's Reading Festival and he confided that he was in with a chance for the Morrissey gig, having been spotted by Alain Whyte. And I was drunk in November when Morrissey played at the Forum in Kentish Town and Spike invited me along. Insobriety again played a part when I saw Spike at a drum 'n' bass night in Camberwell. Like many good drummers, the man is basically a lunatic with a heart of gold. But I suspect the dark heart of the current Morrissey line-up may well reside in enigmatic bassist Gary Day. At first he seems quite suspicious of me, and I'm wary of him because a friend of mine has told me that she used to see him drinking in pubs in Bristol and that she thought he was scary. One of her friends once plucked up the courage to ask him if Morrissey was gay, which he angrily refuted. Today, Gary Day lies on the floor, smoking and picking out the bassline to 'Little Green Bag' by The George Baker Selection on his battered Fender.[118] A member of Morrissey's 'rockabilly' line-up at the start of the '90s, Gary played on the classic *Your Arsenal* album, and features on the *Beethoven Was Deaf* live set, as well as in the *Live In Dallas* video. On those triumphant world tours he alternated between electric bass and the old-fashioned stand-up model that he thrashed and spun and flung around like a dance partner with a death wish. The sight of his wiry limbs heavy with tattoos was quite shocking in those days, when such adornments were still largely the preserve of criminals and career outsiders. Looking like a cross between Matt Dillon and Dirk Bogarde, Gary was the most photogenic of the band, and his image crops up many times in *Morrissey Shot*.

Then he disappeared, to be replaced on later recordings and tours by Johnny Bridgewood. His return seems to signal a desire in Morrissey to recapture what now looks like the golden era of his solo career, although there are no signs of then-drummer Spencer Cobrin returning to the fold.[119]

---

118   Most famously used over the opening sequence of Tarantino's *Reservoir Dogs*.

119   Spencer now fronts his own band. Alain Whyte told me that he was also the original drummer in Bush, who later went on to become the biggest British band in America during the mid-'90s. At the time of writing it appears that LA drummer Dean Butterworth has replaced Spike.

Driving To Manchester At Midnight, Smoking Dope And Listening To 'How Soon Is Now?'

I'm worried because it's very dark and the hire car is full of smoke and, although Gabrielle is a competent driver, she is easily distracted, and she's had a couple of tokes herself. I start to feel a bit trippy, probably because I've smoked on an empty stomach, but the chemical imbalance is certainly enhancing my appreciation of the music. Earlier, when we set off from Bath in daylight, we'd tried to listen to At The Drive In, the hot new American band of the moment, but it just sounded terrible on the car stereo, a real sonic mess.[120] Now, however, 'How Soon Is Now?' is coming alive for me, the tendrils of sound snaking around my head, the pulsing bassline insinuating its way into my bloodstream. I'm reminded of the time in late 1986 when I wandered into the college JCR disco and 'How Soon Is Now?' was playing. I was taken aback because for the first time ever that nondescript room was in possession of an atmosphere. More than that, it was an atmosphere that crackled with menace, hung heavy with the suggestion of forbidden pleasures, and hummed with an electric undercurrent of sex. Not bad for a song about having no friends.

But, of course, 'How Soon Is Now?' is the world's – and definitely America's – favourite Smiths song. There's been a rash of recent cover versions by young post-grunge bands with slacker tendencies. I heard one of these versions on the credits to Charmed, a Buffy The Vampire Slayer rip-off starring Shannen Doherty from *Beverley Hills 90210* that goes out on Channel 5, the UK's home of tacky cult TV. In 2001, Morrissey himself turned up at The Viper Room, the Hollywood club owned by his neighbour Johnny Depp, to see Snake River Conspiracy perform his song.[121] He graciously told singer Toby Torres that her version was better than the original.[122]

---

120   The moment being August 2000. At The Drive In have since split up.
121   A favoured hangout for the LA rock fraternity and their celebrity groupies. The James Dean-like actor River Phoenix died outside the club in 1994.
122   In fact, all the US versions I've heard seem whiny and self-obsessed when compared to the power and despair of the original.

Back To The Old House

When we wake up in Stretford the sun is shining and Rob and Emma have already got the barbecue going, but I'm eager to go sightseeing, to breathe the air that Morrissey breathed when his brain was spewing out the words and melodies of those first Smiths songs. I'm a little puzzled, though, because I'd always imagined Morrissey – or Steve as he was still sometimes known back then – growing up in a world of unbearable negatives. I suppose I thought Stretford would be as bad as Moss Side. Maybe it *was* back in the '70s and early '80s, but in 2000 it's a perfectly respectable lower-middle class neighbourhood. It feels safe and the people seem nice. Personally, I find it hard to see what Morrissey had to be so fucked up about.

After a short walk I'm standing outside number 384 Kings Road. The house. Nobody in possession of the Morrissey surname has lived there since the mid-'80s, but apparently its current lady occupant still receives plenty of mail intended for the singer. Sometimes she opens the letters and scans their contents, bemused. Without the benefit of a forwarding address, she tosses them behind the sofa. Again, it looks like a nice enough house. Morrissey's parents, having emigrated from Ireland, were probably pretty glad to have ended up here, even though this was where their marriage eventually fizzled out. I kind of think there should be some sort of acknowledgement of its former resident. When I lived in London's Belsize Park in 1990, one of the houses in my street bore a blue plaque commemorating the modernist painter Mondrian, which seemed to imbue the whole neighbourhood with a magical atmosphere, the excitement of knowing that someone special lived there.

I'm trying to keep my antennae alert for clues pertaining to Morrissey. Kings Road is a long, wide avenue, which looks like it may once have carried trams. It points towards the town centre a couple of miles away, and Old Trafford is not far. I'd hazard that on match days, the road would have been ablaze with red scarves as the Man U supporters surged towards the stadium. As a youth, Morrissey would have studied them from his bedroom window, or even joined in their throng.[124] His father was a celebrated amateur footballer, and Morrissey himself is known to have attended a few matches as a boy.

Other little things occur to me. When Morrissey referred to himself as 'the last clog in the Arndale Centre' back in the '80s, I'd always assumed he meant the one in the city centre. Now, however, I realise, that there is another Arndale Centre right here in Stretford, a few minutes' walk from the house.[125] A trivial distinction, I suppose, but Morrissey is all about the details. I pay it a visit and slope about, invisible to the obese teenagers and tattooed single mums, and note that the music section in Woolworths does not contain a single recording by Morrissey.

Well, what did I expect? A statue?

---

124   Although Manchester United are arguably the world's greatest football team, most Mancunian musicians seem to make a point of supporting local underdogs Manchester City.
125   Are you getting all this, Mexican–American readers?

DEATH BECOMES HIM: A BANJOLELE–CLUTCHING MORRISSEY GOES SOLO IN A
GRAVEYARD.

Six

Sing Your Life[126]

Critical interpretations of Morrissey's lyrics probably reveal more about the critic than about the author. Certainly, many of his lyrics are pure fiction, Morrissey exercising his creative imagination; others draw on his own life experiences and reflect his various preoccupations. Often, the factual and the fictional merge into one. From what we know about Morrissey's approach to writing, he has worked in a number of ways. His songwriting partnership with Johnny Marr commenced when the guitarist visited him at his home on that mythical day in 1982, whereupon Morrissey produced some words which he had already written.[127] These became the basis of early Smiths songs like 'The Hand That Rocks The Cradle' and 'Suffer Little Children'. Many early Smiths songs have an oddly cumbersome feel to them – lines containing too many or too few lyrics, necessitating peculiar vocal quirks in order to make them scan. As a vocalist, of course, Morrissey is one of the originals. Although much imitated in the '80s, none of his imitators have stayed the distance, and he himself did not copy his style from any famous singers.

This means that he is always recognisable, the Morrissey vocal trademarks being as distinctive in their way as those of Elvis Presley or Frank Sinatra.[128] That said, there were a lot of similar-sounding singers kicking around the UK

126   Morrissey single.
127   Rogan reveals that not only was another person present who was later written out of the Smiths story, but also that Morrissey and Marr had actually met before.
128   Both Kurt Cobain of Nirvana and Evan Dando of the Lemonheads incorporated Morrissey impressions into their performances when appearing on British TV. Comedian Harry Hill portrayed Morrissey on *Celebrity Stars In Their Eyes* and jokingly billed himself as 'Britain's foremost Morrissey impersonator'.

in the early '80s, as punk and the post-punk fallout enticed a generation of misfits out of the bedroom and into the spotlight. Voices which would have been simply too flat, weak, untrained or downright unmusical to cut it in the '60s or '70s were given a chance to shine. Singers like Marc Almond (Soft Cell), Matt Johnson (The The) and Ian McCulloch (Echo and the Bunnymen) all enjoyed success. Punk had loosened up the ears of the record-buying public, and people didn't care that Marc Almond sang 'Tainted Love' out of tune – they loved the song and bought into the raw emotion of the singer's passion-wracked delivery. Morrissey too benefited from the openness of the average music fan's mind at the time. A lot of minor bands were peddling similar dirgy miserablism in the early '80s, but only The Smiths are remembered. But listen to any early '80s compilation and it becomes apparent that, contrary to popular belief, The Smiths had much in common with many of their contemporaries. Johnny Marr's African-sounding guitar on 'This Charming Man' could have been lifted straight off an Orange Juice record, while Tony Hadley's vocals on some early Spandau Ballet material – believe it or not – sound uncommonly similar to Morrissey.

The first Smiths album also won its share of admirers among the legions of goths who haunted the land in those days (they have since returned in force in the service of Marilyn Manson). The gloomy introspection of The Smiths, the midnight-hued tone of the music, not to mention Morrissey's preoccupation with death and depression, all found sympathetic listeners among the children of the hairspray. When Morrissey enjoyed a brief public friendship with Pete Burns – a semi-transvestite goth turned gay/hi-energy disco chart-topper – no one batted a mascara-smeared eyelid.[129] Morrissey's lyric-writing skills had already been appreciated by another Manchester-based guitarist, the much underrated Billy Duffy, who briefly played alongside Morrissey in The Nosebleeds. Duffy later hooked up with an equally charismatic singer, Ian Astbury, in The Cult, and achieved considerable success playing gothic rock that would later mutate into straightforward heavy metal.

129   Despite being a Stock, Aitken and Waterman production, 'You Spin Me Round' was a brilliant record, and deservedly a number one in 1985. Burns and Morrissey even shared the cover of *Smash Hits* and gave an amusing joint interview.

I Think I'm Ready For The Electric Chair[130]

Had their partnership extended further than the two gigs The Nosebleeds played in Manchester in 1978, Duffy's style would have ultimately proved too heavy for Morrissey's sensitive nature. In Johnny Marr, however, the Stretford poet had discovered, or rather been discovered by, his musical soulmate. The mercurial Marr was a conventional musician but an inspired one. He disliked punk but admired such unfashionably workmanlike fare as Bruce Springsteen and Rory Gallagher.[131] In *Mojo* in August 2000, Marr listed his favourite songs, including 'Satisfaction' and 'Gimme Shelter' by The Rolling Stones, 'Metal Guru' by T-Rex and 'Waterloo Sunset' by The Kinks, not to mention tracks by Can, Stevie Wonder, Sly And The Family Stone and James Brown.[132] Prior to his working with Morrissey, Marr had played funk with Andy Rouke in The Freak Party, but his evaluation of that first sheaf of lyrics to what would become Smiths songs led him to undertake a more rock-orientated direction (although a notable funk influence did emerge on a couple of tracks on *Meat Is Murder*). It's interesting to note Marr's fondness for two classic tracks from the beginning and end respectively of The Stones' golden '60s period. Certainly, 'Satisfaction', with its bitingly cynical diatribe on sex, celebrity and consumerism, redefined what it was possible to say in a rock record, while also demonstrating what magic could erupt when a great lyric was welded to a great electric guitar riff. 'Satisfaction' was essentially The Stones attempting to make a soul record and ending up with a new variation on rock. This was a trick that Marr would emulate on 'What Difference Does It Make?', the Smiths' third single, and one of their biggest hits (and reportedly one of Morrissey's least-favourite

130   Early Morrissey song title, recalled by Billy Duffy.
131   The 1987 edition of *The South Bank Show* devoted to The Smiths archly juxtaposed Morrissey's gushing tributes to Manchester punk with an unimpressed dismissal from Marr. Irish guitarist Rory Gallagher has been virtually written out of rock history. Interestingly, one of Marr's greatest riffs, 'Bigmouth Strikes Again' came from another source so unfashionable that few critics would recognise it – namely the '70s incarnation of US soft rockers Heart.
132   Marr appropriated the riff for 'Panic' from 'Metal Guru'. Can were the leading exponents of 'Krautrock' in the '70s, specialising in 'Cosmic German Music'.

Smiths songs). 'Gimme Shelter', on the other hand, was The Stones attempting to make a soul record and instead coming up with an amazingly powerful and haunting amalgam of sci-fi, dustbowl blues-rock and psychedelia. Lyrically, Jagger opted for a timeless, yet sinister, simplicity this time. You could say that 'Gimme Shelter' was to The Stones what 'How Soon Is Now?' was to The Smiths.

The Smiths, of course, always strenuously denied any similarity to the wrinkled rakes of the 'greatest rock 'n' roll band in the world', as it was fashionable to despise The Stones in the '80s. But the similarities – not least in the parallels of the Morrissey and Marr songwriting partnership with Jagger and Richards – are plain to see. Incidentally, Mike Joyce recalls witnessing Mick Jagger dancing at the side of the stage when The Smiths played their first New York show at the Dancetaria on 31 December 1983. Johnny Marr later struck up a friendship with the leather-skinned Keith Richards and even turned to the reptilian rock aristocrat for paternal advice after leaving The Smiths in 1987.

More Songs Than The World Can Stand[133]

After the epiphany of their initial burst of creativity, the songwriting team of The Smiths continued to be impressively prolific for the duration of their short and extremely intense recording career. Morrissey's notoriously awkward personality appears to have made him incapable of working in the traditional manner – bashing out rough ideas with his partner, jamming in the studio, turning up to rehearsals with the germ of a chorus and so on. Instead, the pair evolved an approach similar to the 'two rooms' partnership of pop megastar pianist Elton John and his long-time lyricist Bernie Taupin. Marr would present Morrissey with tapes of instrumental tracks he had recorded; the singer would go away and come up with a set of words and his own typically unique vocal melodies. On at least two occasions, Morrissey could find no lyrical inspiration, and the tracks 'Money Changes Everything'

133   From 'We Hate It When Our Friends Become Successful'.

and 'The Draize Train' were recorded by The Smiths as instrumentals. Possibly as a kind of artistic reprisal, Morrissey insisted on the band recording a number of cover versions against Johnny Marr's better judgement. 'Golden Lights' was originally a hit for '60s poppet Twinkle, while 'Work Is A Four Letter Word' was a Cilla Black song. The former is sweetly slight, appearing on the 1987 US compilation *Louder than Bombs*; the latter is more interesting as, despite its rushed-sounding, ramshackle feel, it actually sounds like a Smiths song, despite Marr's misgivings. On both, it must be noted, Morrissey sings with real feeling. For him at least the two tracks are clearly miniature labours of love.

Enough Is Too Much[134]

After the dissolution of his partnership with Marr – what Rogan refers to as 'the severed alliance' – Morrissey quickly found a new songwriting partner in Smiths engineer and producer Stephen Street, who shyly offered a tape of instrumental compositions to the singer. While no Johnny Marr, Street was a competent guitarist with a good ear for a tune. Unlike Marr, Street favoured the tried and trusted chord sequences of classic pop, resulting in Morrissey's two most successful and best-loved singles, 'Suedehead' and 'Every Day Is Like Sunday' (both 1988), as well as tuneful, affecting B-sides like 'Hairdresser On Fire' and 'Will Never Marry'. Street co-wrote and produced Morrissey's wildly successful debut solo album *Viva Hate* (1988), but the pair fell out over money. After another great single, 'Last of The Famous International Playboys', which hit the UK top ten in February 1989, Street was forced to take action, blocking the release of the 'Interesting Drug' single, until he received the production points he was due for *Viva Hate*. 'Morrissey must have took it that I was trying to screw him', Street told me in 1991, 'and that was it – I was cut off.' The last communication Street received from his former songwriting partner was a postcard inscribed with the words 'Enough is too much' - a quote from 'Interesting Drug'.

---

134   From 'Interesting Drug'.

Off The Rails I Was Happy To Stay[135]

Guitarist Kevin Armstrong partnered Morrissey for the stomping, rent-boy themed 'Piccadilly Palare' single in 1990, and thereafter the singer sought out songwriter Mark Nevin who, with vocalist Eddi Reader in Fairground Attraction, had topped the charts in 1988 with 'Perfect'. Presumably in Fairground Attraction's jazzy, folky acoustic pop, Morrissey detected something of the quaintly English-eccentric, Madness-inspired sound he wanted to pursue.[136] For the *Kill Uncle* album, he drafted in Nevin, Madness bassist Bedders, and Madness producers Clive Langer and Alan Winstanley. Langer co-wrote 'Mute Witness' and 'Found Found Found'; Nevin took the rest. *Kill Uncle* soon entered pop music lore as the worst disaster of Morrissey's career, although in fairness, most Morrissey fans can find five or six songs there to love. Critics seemed obsessed with the fact that the album was short, but its 33 minutes contained ten songs, at least some of them as good as anything on the 1997 Oasis indulgence-fest *Be Here Now*, which lumbered on for an unbearable 40 minutes longer than *Kill Uncle*.[137] Certainly, it seemed strange to attack the man who revived the three-minute pop song for his brevity. As Rogan notes, however, some of the *Kill Uncle* material sounded a lot better live when beefed up by Boz Boorer and co. Certainly, on the *Live In Dallas* video, it's startling to hear 'There's A Place In Hell For Me And My Friends', which ends *Kill Uncle* on a whimpering note, suddenly sounding like a song that certainly thinks it's a classic. At the Wembley and Hammersmith shows in 1991, I remember being impressed by the doomy atmospherics of 'Asian Rut', and positively blown away by the attacking renditions of 'Mute Witness', with Alain Whyte's banshee wail backing vocals. Rogan takes pains to cite 'King Leer' as featuring Morrissey's worst-ever lyric. I have to disagree;

---

135   From 'Piccadilly Palare', palare being the slangy lingo of the homosexual underworld, examples of which are deployed by Morrissey in the song's lyrics.

136   Morrissey's contemporary, pop maverick Julian Cope, also testifies to the godlike genius of Madness. See his memoir *Repossessed* (2000).

137   By common consent, albums today are so long and so packed with filler tracks that virtually nobody listens to them in their entirety any more. However, one of the most exciting releases of 2001, *Your New Favourite Band* by The Hives, was a mere 27 minutes in length.

it's a charming composition, distinguished by the elegant bathos of the final verse ('Your boyfriend, he/ Has displayed to me/ More than just a real hint of cruelty'). Morrissey the unrequited lover is never more self-mocking than here, pathetically proffering a 'homeless Chihuahua' towards the would-be object of his affections. One can almost hear Oscar Wilde, Noel Coward and Kenneth Williams applauding softly during the fade out.

Ultimately, *Kill Uncle* failed not because of its quality, but because of its timing, appearing as it did at the end of the Manchester indie-dance boom and the beginning of the Seattle grunge era. Caught between hedonism on one side and nihilism on the other, Morrissey was simply not of the times in the UK. In America, as has often been noted, it was a very different story.

With his 'rockabilly' band in place – guitarists Boorer and Whyte, bassist Gary Day and drummer Spencer Cobrin – Morrissey found yet another songwriting partner in Alain Whyte, who proved himself adept at a number of styles from glam rock ('Glamorous Glue') to punk-pop (the catchy 'We Hate It When Our Friends Become Successful'). However, it must be pointed out that the two greatest tracks on the album – the strident opener 'You're Gonna Need Someone On Your Side' and the heartrending 'I Know It's Gonna Happen Someday' – were both co-written by the much-derided Mark Nevin. Obliged to send Morrissey tapes of his compositions and receiving no feedback other than floods of cryptic postcards was a frustrating working method for Nevin.[138] 'I just wanted to write songs.' he told *A Chance To Shine* fanzine. 'I wouldn't want to change places with Morrissey. It must be very exhausting and lonely to have that sort of attention.'

Forming a tight unit with his roackabilly boys, Morrissey knocked out a good, solid live album, *Beethoven Was Deaf*, in 1993, featuring nine of the ten songs from *Your Arsenal*. The following year saw the release of *Vauxhall And I*, a fine

---

138   Morrissey also communicated with Siouxsie Sioux in this manner during their collaboration. In August 2002, Siouxsie's partner Budgie told me that Morrissey's highly-distinctive handwriting was very similar to that of Robert Smith from The Cure: 'Really dysfunctional-looking...'

companion to *Your Arsenal*, and a more reflective work than its hard-rocking
predecessor. Curiously, despite the fact that five tracks are co-authored by Boz
Boorer and six by Alain Whyte, the album forms a strongly unified whole,
with little to choose between the writing styles of the two guitarists. Boorer
contributed the gorgeously moving opener 'Now My Heart Is Full', while
Whyte gave us the equally moving 'Hold On To Your Friends'. It's an album
of languorous atmospheres and introspection, with two seaside-themed songs
– Boorer's weirdly haunting 'Lifeguard Sleeping, Girl Drowning' and Whyte's
deliriously sun-drenched 'The Lazy Sunbathers' – sticking in the mind. This is
also Morrissey at perhaps his most cryptically confessional. 'Used To Be A
Sweet Boy' is a painfully lovely song of regret, recalling the boy who held 'so
tightly on to Daddy's hand', while 'Speedway' is simultaneously defiant and
capitulating, ending one of Morrissey's greatest albums with the plaintive
assertion, 'In my own sick way, I'll always stay true to you'.

From this position of strength, Morrissey began to fade from the spotlight,
entering the second half of the '90s with another difficult album, 1995's
Southpaw Grammar, which again has its share of gems if one can be bothered
to make the effort. As ever, Morrissey was well and truly out of step with the
times in terms of the UK music scene, for this was the year of the Britpop
wars between Blur and Oasis, while 1995 also saw the emergence to the
mainstream of trip-hop and what was then termed 'jungle' but is now known
as drum 'n' bass. Against this backdrop, Morrissey chose to release a work
that now sounds like a council estate concept album. To the masses it must
have seemed that Pulp had already effortlessly said all that in one magnificent
single, 'Common People', and yet Morrissey's insights and observations
throw up many fine lyrical moments. The album contains five short songs
and three long ones, but the epic-length opener and closer, 'The Teachers
Are Afraid Of The Pupils' and 'Southpaw' respectively both feel like
standard-length songs with ponderous instrumental sections attached to them
as padding.[139] 'The Operation', meanwhile, reaches its near-seven minutes
length through the addition of a lengthy Spencer Cobrin snare drum solo to

139   Or are we just so used to Morrissey's narrative dominating his songs that we find it
      hard to accept long instrumental passages where his voice does not feature?

the intro. Perhaps Morrissey, wary of finding another *Kill Uncle* on his hands, was desperately attempting to make the work seem more substantial; perhaps he genuinely wanted his musicians to push themselves further.

Whatever his motives, while Southpaw Grammar is one of the least celebrated works in Morrissey's canon, it is certainly the most unusual. Morrissey's voice, once so strident and unashamed, now sounds timid, anxious and defeated, expressing only pain. This syndrome extends also to Morrissey's final album of the '90s, *Maladjusted*, leading me to suspect that he may perhaps have suffered some form of damage to his vocal chords – a common enough danger in his profession. That said, this new voice, though diminished, works well in the context of *Southpaw Grammar*. The most remarkable track is 'The Teachers Are Afraid Of The Pupils'. Exactly ten years after Morrissey sang about the horrors of his schooldays on *Meat is Murder*, he now takes a completely different stance. It is now not malevolent teachers who rule the school, but uncontrollably violent children and their threatening parents. The scenario recalls the short story Mr Raynor The School-teacher in Alan Sillitoe's late-'50s collection *The Loneliness Of The Long Distance Runner*, but this is also an educational scenario, which increasingly plagued British schools in the '80s and '90s. With this one song, laced with menace and the fear of impending violence, Morrissey had finally grown up.

The rest of the songs are pungent snapshots of British yob culture, although 'Best Friend On The Payroll' may refer to Morrissey's typically intense friendship with the volatile but fiercely loyal person known as Jake – who *Select* described as 'a stocky ex-boxer at the 20s-30s crossroads, with a skinhead crop, a white Fred Perry-style shirt and hard blue eyes.' But perhaps the most interesting track is 'Southpaw', with its dreamlike account of a sensitive boy abandoned by his friends; 'so you ran back to Ma/ Which set the pace for the rest of your days'.[140] At the time of writing, Morrissey has no record label, music publishing deal or manager, but his mother is said to be doing his accounts.

---

140   Another theme from *The Loneliness Of The Long Distance Runner*.

Working Girls Like Me[141]

Compilations aside, Morrissey's final album of the '90s was *Maladjusted*, which limped out in 1997 preceded by the apologetic 'Alma Matters' single.[142] Again suffering from *Kill Uncle* syndrome, *Maladjusted* was by no means a bad record, but its appearance generated so little interest that it wasn't until much later that anyone realised it was any good. The opening track is a nightmarish soundscape, sonically reminiscent of Vini Reilley's dentist-drill guitar on *Viva Hate*'s opener 'Alsatian Cousin', with Morrissey's desperate narrative unfolding so gradually that it's only at the very end that it becomes apparent that he has adopted the persona of a female prostitute. Elsewhere, there is the usual tenderness and regret in 'Wide To Receive' and 'Papa Jack', while 'Roy's Keen' is an amusing update of George Formby's famous randy window cleaner.[143] Then there is 'Satan Rejected My Soul', Morrissey's typically idiosyncratic take on the 'me and the devil' theme so prevalent in the history of blues and rock from Robert Johnson onwards. But the album's true gem is 'Trouble Loves Me', which rapidly became an anthem for the few people who actually got to hear it. Someone at Island Records really should have recognised this song's potential and gone out on a limb with a marketing push to secure it its rightful place on the radio and in the charts, because it is truly Morrissey's most commercial moment since 'Everyday Is Like Sunday', nearly a decade earlier. With its Ringo-esque drums and a piano intro reminiscent of Noel Gallagher's borrowings from the John Lennon songbook, 'Trouble Loves Me' is the first time Morrissey has ever given a nod to any artistic influence so obvious and commonplace as The Beatles. It works anyway; the song is uncommonly cherishable, with Morrissey's cracked, imploring vocal, and the quietly beseeching line, 'Down to Soho, oh no/ On the flesh rampage, at your age'. A track as anthemic as this could certainly have crossed over to a mainstream audience, daytime Radio 1, *Top Of The Pops*, *The*

---

141   From 'Maladjusted'.

142   The Latin phrase 'Alma mater' is played on here, while Alma was also the name of a character in the soap opera *Coronation Street* played by the actress Amanda Barrie who starred in *Carry On Cleo*.

143   Roy Keane being a famous Manchester United footballer.

National Lottery Show. But no, it languishes on a forgotten album, and its author has withdrawn to kick his heels in Hollywood; Morrissey's doors are shut to the record companies that never fail to disappoint him.

But the story doesn't end here. When I saw them in rehearsal in January 2000, Morrissey's band members casually mentioned 30 new songs ready to be recorded. By now there could be many more.[144] Morrissey has recently noted the power of the internet in terms of making the music press redundant. He may also be aware of its potential for making record companies redundant. His '80s contemporaries Julian Cope and Matt Johnson (The The), figures even more 'cult' than he, have made themselves self-sufficient on the net, selling both back catalogue recordings and new material. Perhaps it's time Morrissey bought his mother a laptop....

'There's always been a dance element to our music'[145]

The demise of The Smiths coincided with sweeping changes in UK youth culture. From 1987 onwards the public taste shifted from Puritanism to hedonism. The two big new forms of music were house and hip-hop; diametrically opposed and yet curiously parallel. A mutation of '70s disco and European electronica, house was largely lyric-free, aimed squarely at people who didn't want their music contaminated with dreary narratives and tiresome issues (although plenty of political and pseudo-political causes did spring up in connection with the UK dance scene – mainly to do with agitating for the right of clubbers to take drugs and dance whenever and wherever they wanted). House was hailed as a music of liberation – Ecstasy, its drug, promoted a loved-up vibe. Originally the art form of blacks and gays – and black gays – it opened up the social and cultural vistas of many people who were previously straight in every sense of the word.[146] Hip-hop, on the other hand, was distinctly

---

144   New drummer Dean Butterworth played on five new tracks recorded at the end of 2001.

145   The standard protest of all the artists who jumped on the indie-dance bandwagon in '89-'91.

146   See *Altered State* by Matthew Collin and John Godfrey.

homophobic. Unlike the virtually wordless house, this rap-led music was all lyric, an explosion of rage from black America featuring casually violent imagery, extreme misogyny and, ironically, a good deal of racism (mainly directed against whites, Koreans and Jews).[147] Certainly, the ferocious, insanely illogical 'Cave Bitch' by Ice Cube (a 1993 track that ludicrously attacks white hip-hop groupies for being affiliated to the Ku Klux Klan) makes 'Bengali In Platforms' sound like 'Free Nelson Mandela' by comparison.[148]

Hip-hop always contained these tendencies, but there was still a rough-edged innocence to the music in the mid-'80s, and its stomping grooves and punk-like lyrical invective made it a firm favourite among UK music fans – even some of those whose tastes encompassed Morrissey and The Smiths.

As far away as you could possibly get from the cutting edge of the new dance music and hip-hop cultures was the poodle rock which dominated the LA scene in the late '80s, and which in turn would subjugate pretty much the entire world. At the time, a perplexing mutual respect existed between rap groups like Niggers With Attitude and redneck-mentality rock megastars like Guns N' Roses – the idea being that what they shared was an outlaw ethos; they were essentially the same because they shared a nihilistic worldview that precluded them from giving a fuck about anyone or anything. GN'R were reviled in much of the UK music press for vocalist Axl Rose's lame-brained, lowest-common-denominator-nasty diatribe against 'immigrants and faggots' in 'One In A Million'. The same journalists leapt to the defence of NWA whose *Efil 4 Zaggin* (i.e. Niggaz 4 Life) album faced a UK ban owing to the extremity of its lyrical content.[149]

147   When Morrissey portrays himself as a perpetrator of violent acts in songs like 'Is It Really So Strange?', this is the comedy of impotence – it's funny because we can't imagine Morrissey hurting anyone. With a rapper like Ice Cube, or the distinctly psychotic Eazy E (both former members of NWA, the latter now deceased) the effect is more disturbing because these artists are clearly genuinely infatuated with the power afforded to men of violence.

148   Prior to this joyous 1984 hit single by the Special AKA, Nelson Mandela was virtually unheard of in the UK.

149   David Toop, author of *The Rap Attack*, was one of those who helped to lift the ban on the album by testifying on behalf of its artistic and cultural merit.

Back in the UK, the vacuum left by The Smiths naturally left the way open for other bands, many of them from Manchester. Some of these, like The Stone Roses, The Happy Mondays and Oasis, featured members who made unashamedly homophobic comments. With the exception of Morrissey, all the ex-members of The Smiths fitted comfortably into the new Manchester scene of the early '90s.[150] That is not to say that Marr, Rourke and Joyce were homophobic – clearly a ludicrous notion – or that homophobia was ever any kind of driving force or *raison d'etre* for the new bands. No, it was more to do with the fact that these new musicians defined themselves in terms of lad culture rather than art. Any anti-gay comments or anything equally offensive or reactionary could easily be laughed off – just lads on drugs talking shit. The views these men spouted were not to be taken seriously (the gnomic Ian Brown is incapable of making sense; in this he takes his cue from Marley and Dylan, whose delight in perplexing interviewers was gained at the expense of never saying much of value). When Mondays frontman Shaun Ryder casually referred to Radio 1 DJ Jo Whiley as a 'six foot blonde with small tits', he was actually paying her a compliment. The apes had returned from space to rule the planet.

The late '80s UK indie scene certainly needed to lighten up, but these new barbarians ultimately destroyed British rock music as a vital force in world popular culture, bequeathing us the sorry mess we shake our heads over today.[151]

To say the least, truly disappointed[152]

You should never meet your heroes; the disappointment will almost certainly be fatal. That's why, in my own way, I can honestly say I've been avoiding Morrissey for the last 15 years. I think he would appreciate this; he has

---

150   Morrissey's former protégés James, fronted by Tim Booth, enjoyed their greatest success at this time. It was widely assumed that Morrissey's 'We Hate It When Our Friends Become Successful' was directed at them.

151   The music of these bands was largely unexportable, while their attitude was seen as arrogant and unprofessional in the US and elsewhere. In addition, most of the artists burnt out long before they could make a mark outside the UK

152   From 'Disappointed'.

experienced this unique method of self-lacerating illusion-deflation many times. At a late '70s Patti Smith press conference, for example, where the punk poetess's crude language offended his sensibilities; and more recently, when he finally met former New York Dolls frontman David Johansen. Every time he encounters another slack-jawed, wide-eyed fan, Morrissey must feel what it is to be constantly borne back into the past, like F Scott Fitzgerald's boats against the current, and yet he could not resist asking Johansen the questions he'd wanted to ask for almost 30 years. 'Well...' said the old trouper with what must have been infinite weariness. 'It was all a long time ago, y'know?'

So no, you should never meet your heroes. Julie Burchill knows this. She knows it because one morning in 1994 Morrissey, accompanied by press officer Murray Chalmers, turned up at her door, uninvited and without warning (the singer had done the same thing to Sandie Shaw a decade earlier, with happier results). Belying her reputation as Britain's most savagely spiteful writer, Burchill's passion for Morrissey was as pure and untainted as any '70s schoolgirl's devotion to the Bay City Rollers. This all ended the moment she met him, though. Within minutes, she noted, they were sniping at each other like an old married couple who hated each other. The singer and the writer were like two magnets pushed together; essentially the same, they could only repel each other. *The Sunday Times* feature which Burchill subsequently wrote about this odd encounter is one of the strangest and most perceptive accounts of the Morrissey phenomenon, the role-reversal angle being particularly revealing. Usually, in Morrissey's all too rare press encounters, the journalist is ushered into the singer's presence, having been subjected to a gradual disorientation process – cryptic messages, postponed appointments, rescheduled locations. The unsettling stillness of Morrissey in person does the rest. No matter what weapons the journalist musters, Morrissey always controls the room. Not so with Burchill. In a rare instance of an artist invading a journalist's privacy, the Bitch Queen of the UK media was so enraged by her idol that, to clumsily paraphrase Wilde, she decided to exact revenge by effectively killing the thing she loved. If the coward does it with a kiss, and the brave man with the sword, then Burchill alternated with swords and kisses to disembowel the artist she viewed almost as a soulmate.

On that fateful Sunday, the Morrissey camp was reportedly rocked by the published piece, with scary Moz associate Jake taking off on a twelve-mile run to burn off the aggression he felt towards Burchill, darkly stating that if she had been a man she would have received a good kicking from him.

Jake disappeared soon after that, though, while Burchill survived a period of personal and professional turmoil to resurface with a column for *The Guardian* on Saturdays. I think she still loves Morrissey, after a fashion, because she often refers to him, invoking him less as a cultural reference point than as a force of nature, like El Nino or the gravitational pull of the moon. Love like that does not die easily. I should know.

And so, the impossibly sweet pleasure of meeting Morrissey is one which I must avoid. Admittedly, this may well be facilitated by the fact that Morrissey is reputed to roundly despise the vast majority of those who write about him. One of his ugliest lyrics, 'Journalists Who Lie', says it all with sad and rather paranoid brevity. The later 'Reader Meet Author' makes the point with rather more elegance and melody.

In any case, getting to know Morrissey is clearly no easy thing. As he explained to Q in 1989, whenever he encounters anyone who is aware of who he is, any possible exchange is hampered by their perception of him, and by the expectations that stem from this. When interacting with strangers and fans, Morrissey admitted he was handicapped by his sense that they knew infinitely more about him than he could know about them. They had him at a disadvantage, and so he retreated into shyness.[153]

Would Morrissey recognise himself in what I've written about him, in this love letter of a book? Probably not; after all, I'm not really writing about him, but about the things that happen around him, and the debris that trails in his wake. For a man who has spent much of his life in the spotlight, Morrissey is really only ever glimpsed in silhouette. His records are so much more interesting than his life – that is his tragedy. We cannot help loving him anyway – that is ours.

153   Contemporary pop star Moby describes himself as 'an introvert who wants to be an extrovert', a description which can also perhaps be applied to Morrissey.

TRUE TO YOU: A BATTLE-HARDENED MORRISSEY RETURNS IN 1999 AS A
BROODING BRUISER IN A WEST HAM T-SHIRT.

Appendix

James Maker

A writer, musician and film maker, James Maker enjoyed a lengthy friendship with Morrissey, famously dancing onstage with The Smiths at their early gigs. He went on to form the bands Raymonde and RPLA. The following interview was conducted via e-mail in 2001.

Can you tell me the basic details of your early life – date of birth, birthplace, family, education, and so on?

I was born in 1960 at Westminster, London. Apparently I was a complete surprise – the age difference between my sister and I being twelve years. Essentially this meant that she married and left home before I approached puberty, fan worship and bedroom-postering – or should that be bedroom posturing? My father was in the Royal Marines before working in the City and my mother was employed for many years at St. Martin's Theatre in London's West End – strictly an administrative role. Occasionally I'd accompany her there and wander this vast, empty stage and auditorium. It had a comforting, velveteen eeriness to it. I'm probably one of the few people who can watch Lynch's Eraserhead *and think: cosy.*

I attended a grammar school in Surrey from which I was nearly expelled twice. The first time was for habitual absenteeism – I'd been riding a branch line whilst reading Jacqueline Susann's Valley of the Dolls *and* The Well of Loneliness *by Radclyffe Hall. The second occasion was for cutting the uppers of my black patent platform shoes into what I thought resembled a 1940s-style court shoe. I left home at 21, which basted everybody in relief, and went to live on a Peckham housing estate. It was London's South Bronx.*

What were your formative musical and sexual experiences?

Musically, the artist who most interested me was David Bowie. He was a changeling; exotic, intensely stylistic and unpredictable. I liked the urbane glamour of Roxy Music, too. Then came the New York Dolls, who completely dominated my early youth, together with Iggy Pop & The Stooges, Lou Reed and the Velvet Underground, Sex Pistols, Patti Smith, Nico, The Ramones, Sparks, Brian Eno and Talking Heads.

Sexually? I lived in the Kalahari. What consumed me was style, music, literature and being as adolescently self-absorbed as possible. Nothing of a sexual nature happened to me for years – which was astonishing since I had more than a passing resemblance to James Dean. I never went to gay clubs because I couldn't identify with the gay culture that prevailed at the time: disco-divas and clones. Frustration led me to throw myself into the path of oncoming motorcyclists – which isn't really dating.

My first real sexual experience took place within hours of first touching-down at Dallas-Ft. Worth airport – I was stranded there overnight en route to another city and a ranch-hand offered to rent an Eldorado and drive me downtown.

Anything else from the early days you think is significant?

At school, the fashion designer John Galliano and I became friends and accomplices. It seemed to us that the only way to survive the rigours of a repressed, over-disciplined all-boys' school was to imagine it as a women's prison. The best form of defence being attack – we instinctively descended into extortion and semi-sophisticated blackmail. Galliano taught me Spanish, and I taught him how to mangle an Alice Cooper fan's hair into the lathe at Metalwork class. It invested in me the ethos that the only way to deal with adversity is to ignore it. My maxim is this: You've got to grab hold of the tights of life and pull yourself up by the gusset of opportunity.

Did you really telephone Quentin Crisp when you were 13? How did you know about him, how did you get his number, and was it a momentous event in your development?

I telephoned Quentin Crisp after the broadcast of The Naked Civil Servant *– his number was in the phone book. I congratulated him on the film and expressed to him the fact that I was bored to the bottom of my bowels. Any suggestions? He said: 'Try fainting?' Well, to be honest, I'd already exhausted that option. It wasn't a momentous event, but he was very genial. I had lunch with him years later in New York.*

Did you attempt to make contact with any other celebrities?

I wrote to Hylda Baker offering to set up an Appreciation Society in her honour. God knows what I would have filled the Club-letter with had she accepted.

Who did you look up to at this point in your life?

I envied David Johansen his dress-sense, insouciance and Remy Martin wit; Capote, Vidal, Camus, Hubert Selby, Rechy and Baudelaire for their writing. I would also become mildly fixated on deceased British actresses such as Yootha Joyce, Queenie Watts and Margaret Rutherford.

As a teenager, did you have a clear idea of who you were and what you wanted to do?

While a teenager I never had a clear idea of who I was. Teenagedom is experimentation and constant flux. I would variously embrace, reject or customise ideas and opinions to suit my own perspective or view. I was also an inveterate hair-hopper. I knew that my sexual orientation – apart from occasional experiences with girls – was homosexual and I accepted it. My own easy confidence, I think, inspired acceptance in others, too. I never felt confused, ashamed or guilt-ridden on the issue – that would be far too vin ordinaire. *Spiritually, I belong to the Greco-Roman world – not the Christian. I love the violent, colourful imagery of Catholicism, for example; I love its vigour and the inspiration it has brought to art. But I don't hold with its theology or that of any organised religion.*

I knew that my future probably lay in the arts – whether performing or writing or acting. Those passions require a certain degree of introspection. If I were not to do that I'd spend as much of my life as possible travelling – there's a lot out there to see and experience, after all.

The inevitable Morrissey questions... How, when and where did you meet Morrissey? Was he known as 'Steven' or 'Morrissey' then? First impressions?

I had read Morrissey's letters to the NME *in support of the New York Dolls. I phoned him, we talked, and on the strength of that conversation I took the train to Manchester the following weekend. I would have been 16, he 17. The fact that he saw this person wearing an interesting hat emerge from the ticket barrier and didn't bolt was a testament to his nerve. At the time Morrissey looked a little like a Ramone — an intellectual Ramone — if that's possible. He was quietly spoken, considered, somewhat more reserved than I, and very funny. He's always had a very highly developed sense of humour.*

In the mid-'80s, Morrissey recounted in surreal detail a night on the town with you which involved being chased by louts and ending up far from home. The humour aside, was that a true representation of the kind of scrapes you used to get into together?

That story is true. It was like an enduring nightmare and it just went on and on — 'The Manchester Chainsaw Mascara'. We were sat at the window of a restaurant and we'd ordered what, at the time, passed for 'international nibbles'. And these creatures just stood outside on the pavement glaring at us. I remarked: 'If you are what you eat — they probably don't even recognise this food.' On leaving we were chased. We escaped onto a bus and threw coins at them through a window — which incensed them even more. We sat at the back of the bus and, suddenly, the emergency exit door flew open and they unsuccessfully tried to pull me off the bus. We eventually ended up on the Moors and the night grew even stranger...

How did you feel when Morrissey dedicated the New York Dolls book to you?

I was very flattered and very touched.

Explain your role in early Smiths gigs?

I was never Smith No. 5 – nor wished to be. Morrissey invited me to appear with the group at some very early gigs. I did three, I think. My purpose was to wear my quiff, mohair suit and black court shoes and dance in a cool, understated manner. They gave me a pair of maracas for company. And that was it. There was never any question that I'd become a regular fixture.

Had you been involved with music prior to your appearances with The Smiths?

No. Prior to 1984 I hadn't recorded or played live.

In essence, who were you and what were you doing in your late teens and early twenties?

I spent my early twenties feeling as if stranded in the departure lounge of a regional airport – quiet desperation interspersed with dozing. I worked for the Labour Party, after which I tried to immigrate to America. I met a woman from Buffalo for a so-called marriage of convenience. She was perkiness personified. I remember being tapped on the shoulder and looking down to see a small bird-like head atop a pair of novelty leggings. I've always believed that leggings should be eradicated from the planet with Islamic zeal. And the first thing she said was something like, 'Hi! Like 50 per cent don't want Pershing'?

The allure of California suddenly evaporated. I'm a smoker, anyway. I began a love affair with Andalucia instead.

Did you always suspect that Morrissey was capable of doing something extraordinary, or was it a surprise when he achieved notoriety?

I always felt that Morrissey's life would take one of two paths: international pop star or notorious mass murderer.

What were you attempting to do with Raymonde? Was Morrissey influenced by you or were you influenced by Morrissey?

With Raymonde I was essaying the themes in my life – the driving forces of which were love, rage, excess, rage and implosion. I had a deep love and respect of popular music coupled with an abhorrence of the industry. Raymonde felt like pushing outward into risky, alien territory. Progressive, intellectually stimulating at times, but doomed. There were the inevitable comparisons with The Smiths – opinions widely differed. However, it became wearying and tiresome – a rock of Sisyphus – and I felt I had nothing to prove. Morrissey has certainly influenced me in terms of our exchange of ideas and the fact that, at one time, we had an awful lot in common. Whether I have ever influenced him isn't something I could answer.

If you had achieved major success with Raymonde or RPLA, what kind of niche would you have filled? And what, in retrospect, was your Achilles heel?

Niche? Well, I always thought that anybody who had become disillusioned with Anita Harris could always come to us? The niche of Raymonde and RPLA would have been: 'The Group That Nobody Else Likes'. My Achilles heel was a surplus of emotionality with regard to reasoning and perhaps a lack of healthy cynicism in my professional dealings with others.

Are you still close to Morrissey? Do you feel he is misrepresented by what is written about him?

Morrissey and I are no longer close, although our friendship spanned 20 years and I still have a great reservoir of affection for him. Given the particular kind of fan-worship he's inspired, which in many is iconoclastic and fanatical, and the continual rumination on his thoughts, feelings and inner life – I think it's inevitable that he'll be misrepresented. The reason being that Morrissey has still retained his enigma. People love mystery. Part of the process in solving it is projecting your thoughts, feelings and beliefs on to Morrissey and adapting him to the image or person that you want him to be. Which doesn't mean that that's him. In terms of misrepresentation by what is written about him I think: it happens.

Tell me one thing about Morrissey that is not widely known.

He's a very good, plain English cook.

What do you feel was Morrissey's finest moment?

I don't know. There's always the possibility that Morrissey has yet to experience his finest moment?

How crucial was Johnny Marr to the success of The Smiths?

Absolutely crucial. The artistic confluence of Morrissey and Johnny Marr was a very special one. I think of their contribution to popular culture is as significant as that of Lennon/McCartney, Jagger/Richards and Taylor/Burton.

Tell me about Morrissey's approach to sexual politics and gender issues. How do you think he handles the issue of sexual identity in his lyrics.

I think Morrissey's general approach to sexual politics is a broad, pragmatic swathe of common sense that was informed, I think, by the early writings of Germaine Greer and Shere Hite. Personally, I'm not particularly sympathetic to Rousseau or Foucault who constituted the bedrock of '70s feminism. I think contemporary liberalism has been untruthful to women both about men and the world. I'm more of a Sadean who believes that the relationship between the sexes is metaphorically 'combative' in nature – both positively and negatively. On the gender issue Morrissey is in agreement with Gore Vidal's assertion that one cannot be defined as either a heterosexual or a homosexual – there are only heterosexual and homosexual acts. The extension of which is that we are all, ultimately, sexual. Gender-wise, his position is, understandably, non-exclusive. Lyrically, he has written both from a male-to-male, male-to-female and female-to-male perspective. Therein lie the provocation and the enigma.

Acknowledgments

Thank you to: Mike Joyce, Andy Rourke, Gary Day, Spike T Smith and Dean Butterworth for their insights into the Smiths/Morrissey experience. James Maker for his illuminating and witty contribution. Matt Inwood, David Toube and Sue Ellis for reading the manuscript and providing invaluable feedback. Charlotte Morgan for support and patience.

Everyone at www.morrissey-solo.com and all the fans who sent their stories and pictures.

Picture credits

Page 6 © Paul Slattery / RetnaUK / Retna Ltd, US
Page 21 © Paul Slattery / RetnaUK / Retna Ltd, US
Page 33 © Paul Slattery / RetnaUK / Retna Ltd, US
Page 46 © Paul Slattery / RetnaUK / Retna Ltd, US
Page 64 © Lawrence Watson / RetnaUK / Retna Ltd, US
Page 71 © Lawrence Watson / RetnaUK / Retna Ltd, US;
Page 87 © Luis Sinco / Los Angeles Times / Distributed by Retna Ltd, USA

All photographs courtesy of Retna Images. Absolute Press would like to thank Kerri Mathes and the team at Retna for their generous assistance in compiling the images for this book.

Outlines

Chronicling the lives of some of the most exceptional
gay and lesbian artists of the last century.

Available from all good bookstores or orders directly to Absolute Press.
Send cheques (payable to Absolute Press) or VISA/Mastercard details to:
Absolute Press, Scarborough House, 29 James Street West, Bath BA1 2BT.
Phone 01225 316 013 for any further details or visit the website at
www.absolutepress.co.uk